AF407483

Cherished

with
Love from Above

Danny Frigulti

Dedication

This book is written to all the people in the world so that they might have a proper understanding of how God's love has been revealed to all humanity since the beginning of His creation.

Acknowledgements

Special thanks to Dave, Sam, Randy, and Mary for proofing, editing, suggestions, cover design by Chuck Romer, and Larry with website help. Also, thanks for prayer support from Kent, Jaymes, Tommy, Diane, Jan, and the many who encourage me.

Bible Versions Used:

The 1988 King James Study Bible, second edition, published by Thomas Nelson, is the primary Scripture reference. Some, who are not familiar with the King James language format, find certain words and phrases difficult to understand. Therefore, in order to explain certain verses, I use a combination of words from other translations for adding clarity to what is being presented. The words I use to explain and describe the events are not intended to be misleading. The Hebrew and Greek language resource books (commentaries and concordances) are cited to elucidate the text. I have used these sources for over thirty years to develop a better understanding of the true inspiration of Scripture that was preserved for our benefit. Some verses from the New American Standard Bible (Open Bible, Expanded Edition, 1985, by Thomas Nelson) are quoted. Also, Bible Search and Study Tools – Blue Letter Bible is used.

ISBN — 9798652739560

Author's website: www.dannyfrigulti.com

Other books by the author are available at **Amazon.com**

The heavens declare the glory of God; and the firmament shows His handiwork (Psalm 19:1, KJV).

He has made everything beautiful in its time. Also, God has set eternity in our hearts that we might know Him during this life and in heaven. Yet, men and women will not find out all the work God has done from the beginning to the end (Ecclesiastes 3:11).

Table of Contents

Lovingkindness and truth have met together;
Righteousness and peace have kissed each other.
(Psalm 85:10, NASB)

Opening Comments

While listening to music on my computer, a certain song I had not heard for years captivated my attention. That song is titled *Cherish* and was recorded in 1966 by a group called The Association. The melody and words display truth and beauty. As I listened to it repeatedly, the idea for this book began forming in my mind. Take time to listen to *Cherish*, and you will realize that we do not cherish one another in friendships and marriage as often as we should.

Since "cherish" is the word of focus in this book, it is a must to present a common definition of this precious word so that we can realize our need to activate the definition daily in various relationships. To cherish someone is to:

> hold dear, treat tenderly with care and
> affection, keep in mind, cling to in thought

I have memorized the meaning of "cherish" and have asked God for His help in living out this word so that people will be edified and blessed when we share conversation. Our world would be a much better and safer place if this word was taught to us from the time we were in diapers with role models to follow.

Also, words such as "precious," "beloved," and "treasure" should describe the way we treat people daily. Taking time to look at the definitions of these words will show applications of these vital concepts are needed worldwide for improving relationships. These important words are interlinked with similar meaning. When we take time to examine our words and deeds regularly, it becomes clear that we can improve.

We are all looking for love and acceptance in marriage and friendships. Our journey of historical evidence will guide us to love and acceptance that lasts forever, a love that was prepared for us by "The Lord of Love," our caring Creator.

After years of research and discussions with people, I am convinced the Bible has the most detailed information about how God cares for people. Therefore, an emphasis on Biblical examples that prove He cherishes us are presented from chapter to chapter. Evidence confirms that the recorded history in the Bible consistently reveals an unbroken plan from God to cherish us. We are His beloved.

From Genesis to Revelation, there is a continuous pattern of "love from Above" that resonates with the evidence that He intervenes personally in and through our lives. Scripture will show how His "love from Above" enters the hearts of people who want it. Historical accounts will give details of how God has loved people since He created the world.

Years ago, I heard a speaker say "The Bible is God's love letter to us." This is an accurate statement and will become evident as you read through this book. Writings from the prophets and the apostles of Jesus will prove we are His prized possession. Thus, a plan of forgiveness for our sins is God's love-plan so that we have no guilt when we enter Heaven.

Forthcoming chapters will divulge pieces of information that will open up your mind and heart for understanding and receiving His love. Numerous verses of Scripture reveal God's guidance, protection, blessings, and rewards. They verify we have always been in the cross-hairs of His love.

When you have finished reading the details of God's love for humanity, you will see He had a plan to personally cherish us with love for eternity. His plan to cherish us includes people of all beautiful skin colors, because He made our different skin colors. Thus, those of different nationalities and languages can accept His love and proclaim His grace and forgiveness with confident joy.

Earthly and heavenly fellowship with God brings joy and delight to Him and to us. He literally rejoices over those who desire for Him to enter their heart with His Holy Spirit, so that He would call them "His cherished beloved." Then He will continually prove His cherish-filled love for them.

The fact-filled spiritual journey of God's plan to love and cherish us for now and for eternity is a heavenly pattern that is designed for all. Hopefully, you will be captivated with the thought of being cherished forever. Respond to His desire to shower you with blessings and always be with you. His desire is to leave His legacy of love in your heart.

If you memorize the definition of "cherish," as you read, the information should be more heartwarming.

Revealed glory speaks forth a beautiful creation.
Our God has prepared an eternal love foundation.
His heart's concern was that mankind not perish.
The Son of God revealed how God would cherish.

1

Cherish Begins in
the Garden of Eden

As we start our spiritual journey to establish that we are "cherished with love from above," historical facts are needed. From the beginning of humanity, there are preserved documents which provide information about the first people mentioned in human history. The oldest discovered *and* detailed documents about the beginning of humanity are found in the Bible. So I use this information to establish a foundation of cherish and love facts.

The first book of the Bible is Genesis and gives details about the creation of the world. A step-by-step process of how everything was created is recorded in the first two chapters of Genesis, including mankind.

There are two verses (Genesis 1:26-27) that deserve a close inspection to confirm that God created us unique, specifically for the purpose for reciprocating verbal contact. Let's take a close look at these two verses and realize, from the beginning of humanity, our Creator was careful to make us in His image so we could love each other. They read:

[26]And God said, Let Us make man in Our image, after Our likeness: and let them have dominion over the fish of the sea, and over the fowl of the air, and over the cattle, and over all the earth, and over every creeping thing that creeps upon the earth.

[27]So God created man in His *own* image, in the image of God created He him; male and female created He them (KJV).

From these verses our attention will focus on two words, "image" and "likeness," to understand how God is determined to have a personal relationship with all people. This conveys that He desires to cherish us in various ways. Also notice that the phrase "*after* Our likeness" is recorded, not "*and* Our likeness." There is a reason for this. These two Hebrew words (image, likeness) work together to describe how God made us spiritually inside our physical body. They have a specific purpose we need to understand which helps us realize why we were created.

In John 4:24, Jesus said "God is spirit." God does not have a physical body as we do. "Image and likeness" are words that are used in a synonymous manner to emphasize that our inner person is spirit. "Image and likeness" give us our personality and enable us to communicate with our Creator Who shaped, formed, and patterned our spirit to have direct communication with Him. God's spiritual image is engraved within us that we might know Him for the purpose of receiving His love, guidance, comfort, and forgiveness for all wrongs committed. In return, we are to love and forgive as God forgives us.

Since God created His image in man, this means man's spirit had a beginning and is not eternal. God is eternal. Nowhere in the Bible does it teach that being made in God's image means we are divine beings. Therefore, it is wrong to believe and teach that we all have a spark of eternal divinity in us from conception or birth.

Genesis 2:7 says God created man from the dust of the ground. Some people reject the recorded fact that Adam was formed from the dust of the ground. They just don't think it's possible for the eternal Creator to do such a thing. However, when one looks back in Genesis 1 and sees that God spoke and created all things that had never existed into existence, it would be easy for Him to use dust and form or fashion a human being of His desire.

Verse 8 says the LORD God planted a garden eastward in Eden and put the man (Adam) in it. When we get to verse 20, we find that Adam needed a helper. Let's look at verses 21-23, for they describe how the first woman came into being:

> 21And the LORD God caused a deep sleep to fall upon Adam, and he slept: and He took one of his ribs, and closed up the flesh instead thereof;

> 22And the rib, which the LORD God had taken from man, made He a woman, and brought her unto the man.

23And Adam said, This *is* now bone of my bones, and flesh of my flesh: she shall be called Woman, because she was taken out of Man.

24Therefore, shall a man leave his father and his mother, and shall cleave unto his wife: and they shall be one flesh (KJV).

Adam came from the dust of the ground, and his helper, who would be called Eve (Genesis 3:20), came from one of his ribs. She did not come from his feet to be looked down upon. Coming from his side denotes equality to work together. When working together is practiced between a man and a woman in a marriage, a completely healthy relationship is formed that produces mutual respect, trust, and admiration.

Another important fact we must not overlook is that Eve not only is of the same flesh and bone as Adam, but she is also of the same inner spiritual nature as Adam. She is created in the "image of God, after His likeness" (verses 26-27). This means, from the beginning of human creation, man and woman *are equal* and precious in God's eyes and heart.

As we look at chapter 3 in Genesis, clarification on a misunderstood belief about the Garden of Eden and Adam and Eve needs our attention. Some people believe that Adam and Eve were not literal people, and the story of temptation in the Garden never happened. However, a famous and often quoted first century Jewish historian named Flavius Josephus recorded that for centuries this historical Garden of Eden account was accepted as truth from the beginning of mankind.

Cherish Begins in the Garden of Eden

A book titled *Complete Works of Flavius Josephus* contains this information. It presents clear and dogmatic details about Adam and Eve, as well as the Garden of Eden.[1] His teaching is part of the Jewish heritage and was taught as a literal historical account that occurred thousands of years ago. To date, no reliable Jewish source that teaches otherwise has surfaced.

The Garden of Eden account occurred thousands of years *before* Moses led the Hebrews out of 400 years of Egyptian bondage. Moses wrote the details of Genesis about 1,400 B C. In recording the Hebrew language and mankind's history to the people, Moses would not have started the beginning of God's creation with information that was not literal.

Centuries later, with confidence, Jesus quoted the Genesis 2:24 record literally in Mark 10:6-8. Therefore, Jesus believed the Genesis account of humanity was just as Moses recorded. Chapter 3 of Genesis reveals how sin came into the world, and the consequences of the beginning of man's sin. Several verses, from the beginning of the chapter, help us to understand what sin is and to know the problems it causes.

> [1]Now the serpent was more subtle than any beast of the field which the LORD God had made. And he said unto the woman, Yea, hath God said, Ye shall not eat of every tree of the garden?
>
> [2]And the woman said unto the serpent, We may eat of the fruit of the trees of the garden:

³But of the fruit of the tree which *is* in the midst of the garden, God hath said, Ye shall not eat of it, neither shall ye touch it, lest ye die.

⁴And the serpent said unto the woman, Ye shall not surely die:

⁵For God doth know that in the day ye eat thereof, then your eyes shall be opened, and ye shall be as gods, knowing good and evil.

These five verses reveal, that in the beginning of the human race, there were two people created by God, and they were living in a garden. They were told they could eat from every tree in the garden except one that was in the midst of the garden (verse 3). They were not to touch or eat from this specific tree or death would occur (Genesis 2:15-17).

The serpent is mentioned in verse 1, and we are told that he talks. The Hebrew word for "serpent" can also be translated "snake." So, is this an actual talking snake who is conversing with Eve? Or is this a description and title of an actual creature that will be shown throughout Scripture to be an enemy of God? The serpent was Satan, an enemy of God, with an agenda to derail God's love for humanity.

This creature had an intelligent awareness of what God had said to Adam and Eve about the forbidden tree. Reptiles do not possess such knowledge. Also, verse 1 says the serpent was more subtle (cunning, crafty) than any beast of the field. Animals are extremely cunning and crafty when pursuing what their appetite desires. But this serpent had an appetite to deceive God's most prized creation, those who were created in the image of the Almighty God. This wicked being is jealous of God and hates Him.

To identify who this cunning liar and deceiver is, we can look at other verses where the serpent is mentioned. In 2 Corinthians 11:3, the serpent is labeled as the one who "beguiled Eve through his craftiness." This refers specifically to the incident in the Garden of Eden.

Moving to The Book of Revelation, we see more verses that give us a clear picture proving the identity of the serpent. Revelation 12:9 says "the great dragon was cast out, that old serpent, called the Devil and Satan, who deceives the whole world." In this verse, we see that the serpent is also known as the great dragon, the Devil, and Satan.

Revelation 20:2 tells us, "And he laid hold on the dragon, that old serpent, which is the Devil, and Satan, and bound him for a thousand years" (KJV). Scriptures make it clear that the serpent in the Garden of Eden was not a snake that slithers on the ground, but one known as the Devil and Satan. Therefore, it is accurate to label this talking serpent, not as a snake that slithers on the ground and in trees, but rather the Devil who deceived Eve to disobey the LORD.

> 6And when the woman saw that the tree *was* good for food, and that it *was* pleasant to the eyes, and a tree to be desired to make *one* wise, she took of the fruit thereof, and did eat, and

gave also unto her husband with her; and he did eat.

7And the eyes of them both were opened, and they knew that they *were* naked; and they sewed fig leaves together, and made themselves aprons.

8And they heard the voice of the LORD God walking in the garden in the cool of the day: and Adam and his wife hid themselves from the presence of the LORD God amongst the trees of the garden.

9And the LORD God called unto Adam, and said unto him, Where *art* thou?

10And he said, I heard thy voice in the garden, and I was afraid, because I *was* naked; and I hid myself.

11And He said, Who told thee that thou *wast* naked? Hast thou eaten of the tree, whereof I commanded thee that thou shouldest not eat?

12And the man said, The woman whom thou gavest *to be* with me, she gave me of the tree, and I did eat.

13And the LORD God said unto the woman, What *is* this *that* thou hast done? And the woman said, The serpent beguiled me, and I did eat.

Cherish Begins in the Garden of Eden

> ¹⁴And the LORD God said unto the serpent, Because thou hast done this, thou *art* cursed above all cattle, and above every beast of the field; upon thy belly shalt thou go, and dust shalt thou eat all the days of thy life:
>
> ¹⁵And I will put enmity between thee and the woman, and between thy seed and her seed; it shall bruise thy head, and thou shalt bruise his heel.

Verse 15 sends an ongoing message to humanity that cannot be ignored. God is putting enmity (mutual hatred) between the seed of the woman and the seed of the serpent. What does this statement mean in reference to the two seeds that will have hatred for each other? It means one seed line will follow the holy God and the other will follow the evil serpent. Therefore, many centuries of war with spiritual and physical consequences will confront each other throughout history, as is evident today.

In human reproduction, the seed refers to the man, not the woman. Roman's 5:12 says by one man (Adam), sin entered the world and sin has been passed on to all. In Psalm 51:5, King David records, "I was brought forth in iniquity; and in sin did my mother conceive me" (KJV).

Isaiah 7:14 is a "cherish prophecy" of redemption given hundreds of years in advance to alert man that God will send His Son to be born of a virgin. This will allow His Son to give Himself as a sacrifice for our sins (Ephesians 1:7, 13-14).

Thus, this One born of the virgin shall be born with no sin passed on to Him. Micah 5:2 cites a specific place of birth to notify mankind that a specific Person will come to redeem us from our sins and reconcile us to God. This verse confirms that God had a plan to provide forgiveness for all of man's sins.

The seed of the serpent represents those who will reject God's forgiveness and follow Satan and his legions of evil spirits. Those who do not accept God's forgiveness continue to walk under "the prince of the power of the air" (Ephesians 2:2).

[16]Unto the woman he said, I will greatly multiply thy sorrow and thy conception; in sorrow thou shalt bring forth children; and thy desire *shall be* to thy husband, and he shall rule over thee.

[17]And unto Adam He said, Because thou hast hearkened unto the voice of thy wife, and hast eaten of the tree, of which I commanded thee, saying, Thou shalt not eat of it: cursed *is* the ground for thy sake; in sorrow shalt thou eat *of* it all the days of thy life;

[18]Thorns also and thistles shall it bring forth to thee; and thou shalt eat the herb of the field;

[19]In the sweat of thy face shalt thou eat bread, till thou return unto the ground; for out of it wast thou taken: for dust thou *art*, and unto dust shalt thou return.

20And Adam called his wife's name Eve; because she was the mother of all living.

21Unto Adam also and to his wife did the LORD God make coats of skins, and clothed them.

22And the LORD God said, Behold, the man is become as one of Us, to know good and evil: and now, lest he put forth his hand, and take also of the tree of life, and eat, and live forever:

23Therefore the LORD God sent him forth from the Garden of Eden, to till the ground from whence he was taken.

24So He drove out the man; and He placed at the east of the Garden of Eden, Cherubims, and a flaming sword which turned every way, to keep the way of the tree of life.

A careful reading of these verses in Genesis 3 gives us insight to the first recorded instance where humans chose not to obey God's instruction concerning what to do and what not to do. Though Adam and Eve were given plenty of fruit to eat from various trees in the garden, they chose to disobey God's one guideline, which was not to eat of the tree in the middle of the Garden (verses 1-7).

Man's result of rebelling against God's guideline was being "driven out of the Garden" (verse 24). This act of rebellion, also known as sin, brought death (verses 3-4, 19), and man could no longer talk audibly face to face with his

Maker on a regular basis. Despite man's defiance of God's only Garden guideline, he would still be cherished.

The story of humanity's beginning has multiple lessons for us. We were created with free will, which means we can follow God's way or chart our own way. It also reveals that there is an enemy (the Devil) who hates God and desires to tempt humanity to go against God's instructions by getting people to doubt the truth of His words.

Since we are created in God's spiritual image for a relationship with Him, the Devil works at persuading us to reject God's words and ways of truth. When this is achieved, we put communication distance between us and our Creator, which is what happened with Adam and Eve. They could have called out to the LORD for help but chose to do their own thing, and it was costly.

The Serpent's beguiling words of seduction and deception have continued to describe his historical earthly lifestyle as recorded in Matthew 4:3 and 1 Thessalonians 3:5 where he is identified as "the tempter." The Devil and his legions of evil spirits constantly tempt humanity to reject the Bible, because it is filled with wisdom that teaches us to accept God's ways for blessings and eternal love.

Despite man's fall into sin, which put distance between God and man, the LORD had prepared an eternal forgiveness plan. Revelation 13:8 mentions "the Lamb of God slain from the foundation of the world." From the beginning of creation, God knew people would sin, so He set up a way to forgive all sins (John 1:29) proving He would cherish us.

Forthcoming chapters will show that despite how much people like to rebel against God's instruction, He will keep His eye on them to express His nature of love and forgiveness. His desire to cherish us will be shown. It is important to remember that the words "love" and "beloved" are mentioned over a hundred times in the Bible. He loves us, and we are His beloved. We are precious to Him, for we are His unique heavenly treasure chest of fellowship.

Endnote:

1. William Whiston, *Complete Works of Flavius Josephus* (Grand Rapids, Michigan, Kregel Publications, 1978), p. 25.

Leaving the Garden is the dawning of a new day.
Exploring His creation brings a bright new way.
People will multiply and rejoice in their treasures.
Yet some forget the One Who provides pleasures.

2

More People to Cherish

Chapters 4-11 in Genesis describe how humanity began to spread around the world. Numerous names and lineages are recorded, and unusual events are presented to help us realize that people make good and bad decisions. Romans 15:4 tells us that "the former things were written for our learning that through the patience and comfort of the Scriptures, we might have hope." Stories in Old Testament history reveal God's plan to love and cherish mankind.

The first story is about a husband and wife, Abram and Sarai. Genesis 16:1 reveals that Sarai had not been able to bear a child. This caused her much grief, but God had a plan. When the LORD appeared to Abram at age 99 (Genesis 17:1), He changed their names to Abraham and Sarah (Genesis 17:5-6, 15). In verse 16, God told Abraham He "will bless Sarah and give her a son."

Abraham was so stunned that he fell on his face and laughed, saying in his heart "Shall a child be born unto him that is a hundred years old? And shall Sarah, that is ninety years old, bear?" (KJV). When Sarah heard about her bearing a child at her age, she laughed and said "shall I have pleasure in my old age?" (Genesis 18:11-12).

The LORD heard her response and replied, "Is anything too hard for the LORD?" He said He would return at the appointed time, and Sarah would have a son (verse 14). At the right time, Sarah bore a son named Isaac (Genesis 21:1-3). Isaac fathered a son named Jacob (Genesis 25:19-26). This family line of Abraham, Isaac, and Jacob would establish a chronological line from which the Messiah (Christ) came, the One Who would forgive the sins of the world.

Both were advanced in age, when people don't think about starting a family, yet God chose to bless them. This blessing would turn out to prove God cherishes all people, because we are all created in His image for the purpose of also cherishing our caring Creator. Eternal love and forgiveness were predestined to come through Abraham's seed, because one day a sin-free man would be born from his line. That man was more than a man. He is known as Jesus, the Son of God.

God was merciful to Abraham and Sarah with a miracle. I have heard of more than one story where a couple was told they would not be able to have children. They prayed and God answered with a miracle that defied medical understanding. "With God, all things are possible" (Matthew 19:26). The God of Abraham, Isaac, and Jacob has become known around the world for thousands of years as the true God.

The story of Joseph and his multi-colored tunic (robe) has been acted out many times in churches over the years. We pick up the story in Genesis 37:3 where we find that Israel (i. e.,

Jacob), Joseph's father, loved him more than all of his sons. This stirred up jealousy and caused hatred from his brothers (verse 4), and they plotted to kill him (verses 18-20).

Also, Joseph was given two dreams in which it was revealed to him that he would reign over his older brothers, and they would bow down to him in the future (verses 5-11). These dreams intensified the animosity from his brothers.

When Joseph came to see them in the fields, his brothers stripped him of his tunic of many colors and threw him into an empty pit but made a decision not to kill him. Instead they set it up to have him sold for twenty shekels of silver to the Ishmaelites (verses 23-28). Then they came up with the idea to make it look like a wild beast had attacked and killed Joseph. They slaughtered a male goat and dipped the tunic into the blood to make it appear that a wild beast had killed Joseph and showed it to their father (verses 31-33).

Joseph was taken to Egypt where he was sold as a slave to Potiphar, an Egyptian officer of Pharaoh, but Joseph was not forgotten by the LORD. The LORD was with him and he became successful, for all he did brought prosperity. The result of his success brought blessings to the Egyptians (Genesis 39:1-6).

As a handsome man in form and appearance, Potiphar's wife was very attracted to Joseph. His master's wife tried to seduce him day after day, but Joseph strongly resisted (verses 7-10). Then came a day when she pulled his garment from him, and he fled from the house where he was working, and she made it look like Joseph tried to seduce her (verses 11-16).

When Potiphar heard the lie about Joseph trying to seduce her, he believed his wife. He had Joseph thrown into prison. However, the LORD had compassion on Joseph and later gave him favor and prosperity with Pharaoh when Pharaoh sought Joseph's prophetic insight concerning dreams (Genesis 41:14-46). God was determined to see that the previous prophetic dreams He gave to Joseph would happen for His glory.

Chapter 41 again proves Joseph is prophetically gifted to interpret dreams while in prison. This shows God was always with him no matter what his circumstances. As time went on, Pharaoh was given a dream about seven fat cows and seven gaunt cows. He fell asleep and had a second dream where he saw stalks of good corn and other stalks of corn that were scorched by an east wind (verses 1-7).

Pharaoh was deeply disturbed by these dreams and asked for his magicians and wise men to interpret them, but none could (verse 8). Joseph's gift of interpretation was made known to Pharaoh, and he was summoned from prison. Pharaoh told Joseph his dreams, and Joseph gave him God's exact meaning of the dreams (verses 15-37). There would be seven years of crop abundance, then seven years of famine.

This came to pass and the Egyptians had food, but other nations suffered during this time. Joseph was placed in charge of Egypt to make sure the grains were stored during the plentiful years, and he remained faithful to the true God Who had blessed him (verses 50-52). He had no idea that the LORD had a great surprise for him, and it would be revealed through his family he had not seen in decades.

More People to Cherish

As the famine began in the lands around Egypt, countries came to Egypt to purchase grain (verse 57). Jacob, Joseph's father, sent ten of his sons to Egypt to buy grain, but Benjamin did not go (Genesis 42:1-4). When Joseph's brothers arrived in Egypt and came before him, they did not recognize Joseph. But he recognized them and remembered his dreams of long ago (verses 5-9). They bought grain and headed home.

Extensive details about this encounter continue through chapters 42-44 that reveal a second trip was made to Egypt. Take time to read these chapters. In Genesis 45:1-15, Joseph began weeping, disclosed who he is to his brothers, and kissed them. He had no ill will toward his brothers for what they had done to him in his earlier days. He asked how his father was doing and soon his entire family moved to Egypt.

When this story comes to an end, Joseph spoke words of forgiveness to his brothers that are beautiful. These are words we should all remember.

> And as for you, you meant evil against me, but
> God meant it for good in order to bring about
> this present result, to preserve many people
> alive (Genesis 50:20, NASB).

This true story teaches us that when God puts a dream in a person's heart, He will cherish that person and bring it to pass, no matter how many years go by. It also teaches us to remain faithful to the LORD, and in time He will bless us and others around us. And it teaches us to forgive those who have wronged us, to keep busy in doing what God has gifted us to do, and to not get bitter because things don't always go smoothly for us.

After Joseph passed away, a new Egyptian ruler came into power. He did not treat the Israelites well. A Hebrew baby named Moses would grow up in the Egyptian empire and become a prominent man in Egypt. Later in his life, he would cling to his Hebrew heritage (Exodus 2:1-15) and leave Egypt.

God placed Moses in charge when the Israelites were led out of Egypt (Exodus 3:10). During their journey, God would give them a list of what is known as The Ten Commandments to obey. The purpose was to let them know what pleased God and what didn't. These commandments told the people what was sinful to God and what was holy to God. These are listed in Exodus 20:1-17.

Rather than list them, I would encourage you to take the time to read through these 17 verses. If people around the world, whether religious or not, would follow these directions, our world would have better family life, less crime, more respect, more love for each other, and more peace.

Moses had a sister named Miriam. She was a prophetess, singer, and dancer according to Exodus 15:20-21. Miriam and all the women went out with timbrels and dances to glorify the LORD, for He had led them through the Red Sea (Exodus 14:21-15:19).

God cherished them with miraculous protection, and these wonderful women cherished Him with songs of praise, dances of joy, and noisy timbrels. A true God-appointed prophetess,

Miriam heard from God just as a male prophet hears from the Almighty.

There is another lady of prominence who deserves honor. Her name is Deborah. She was a prophetess and judge of Israel (Judges 4:4-5). Like Miriam, she sang praises to the LORD for protecting the people (Judges 5:1-31). Judging situations and people properly is not always easy. But God blessed this woman with a special position of wisdom and authority.

In the New Covenant, we find that God still appoints women in a prophetic role. In Acts 2:17-18, Peter records that "your daughters and hand maidens shall prophesy." This is a quote from Joel 2:28. And Acts 21:9 says a "man had four daughters, virgins, which did prophesy" (KJV).

The next chapter features more memorable ladies from different backgrounds. These precious women would have great historical impact.

Trusting to receive God's heavenly touch,
Women from different cultures leave so much.
Some friends would lead them to His Name,
And their new lifestyle would never be the same.

3

Some Ladies to Cherish

After Moses passed away, Joshua was chosen to guide and lead the Israelites to God's Promised Land (Deuteronomy 34:9). Previously, the Israelites had faced strong opposition from demon-worshipping nations that did not care about the God of Israel. Yet, the word of His power that had destroyed the Egyptian empire had gone before them. The ten plagues that crushed the great Egyptian era are found in Exodus 7-12 and nations heard of this conquering power, as well as victories over other cities (Joshua 2:9-11).

The story of the city of Jericho is amazing. Joshua sent two spies into the land to see the fortifications. They ended up being sheltered in a house where a harlot named Rahab lived (Joshua 2:1). Some people in Jericho saw the strangers enter their city and told the king of Jericho. Men came to Rahab's house to find the two Israelites, but she said they had left. However, Rahab had hidden them in the stalks on the roof (verses 2-6).

Before the two spies had left, Rahab shared her people's fear that they had about the God Who led Israel out of Egypt (verses 8-11). After confessing the great power of the LORD their God, she asked them to spare her family from death when the Israelites attacked Jericho.

More wise conversation followed, and Rahab was given specific instructions to follow for safety. She was told to tie a scarlet cord in the window through which she had let the men down. When the city was attacked, the people who were in the house with the scarlet cord in the window would be spared (verses 12-21).

The words of Rahab confirmed she had placed her faith in the God Who guarded His people and brought them safely out of Egypt. When Israel assaulted the city (Joshua 6:1-22), she and her household were saved from harm and death. Also, her relatives were brought out to safety (verse 23), and all of her household continued to live in Israel (verse 24).

Rahab is remembered as a faithful servant of the true God. Over a thousand years later, the writer of Hebrews 11:30-31 mentions her faith in a chapter that recognizes unique men and women who impacted holy history. Rahab was an example of a woman who had an open and dedicated heart to the LORD Who gives love, forgiveness, and protection. She cherished God, and He cherished her. We need more wonderful and precious women like Rahab.

For centuries, the love story of Ruth and Boaz has been a favorite of many. Let's take a look at it and enjoy this special love story that unites people of different backgrounds for God's glory. The word "kinsman" is important for us to remember in this heart-warming narrative. Kinsman carries the

the meaning of "one who redeems." The redemption can refer to property or a person, and in this case, it is both.

Starting at chapter 1, we are told there was a great famine in the land. So Elimelech of Bethlehem, his wife, Naomi, and their two sons, Mahlon and Chilion, went to the land of Moab and remained there. Elimelech died. The Moabites did not worship the true God of Israel. They worshipped other gods. Still, the two sons took Moabite women for wives. One was named Orpah and the other Ruth. The family was there about ten years, and the sons died, leaving widows (verses 1-5).

Naomi heard the LORD had blessed her homeland with food and wanted to return, so she prepared to return to the land of Judah (verses 6- 7). She told her daughters-in law that they should stay in their land and not go with her. Both women wanted to go with Naomi, but eventually only Ruth went with Naomi. To show how determined Ruth was in her desire to go with Naomi, she told Naomi the following:

> [16]But Ruth said, "Do not urge me to leave you or turn back from following you; for where you go, I will go, and where you lodge, I will lodge. Your people shall be my people, and your God, my God. [17]"Where you die, I will die, and there I will be buried. Thus may the LORD do to me, and worse, if anything but death parts you and me." [18]When she saw that she was determined to go with her, she said no more to her (NASB).

Their trip took them to Bethlehem at the barley harvest time, which would prove to be a blessing they did not expect (verse 22).

In chapter 2, the connection between Ruth and Boaz begins to unfold. Naomi knew a man of great wealth named Boaz. He was a kinsman of her deceased husband. Ruth wanted to work, and went to glean in the fields owned by Boaz (verses 1-3). He saw her and inquired about her. He was pleased with her desire to work, and told her to stay in his field (verses 5-9).

Ruth was filled with thankfulness and bowed down before Boaz saying, "Why have I found favor in your sight that you should take notice of me, since I am a foreigner?" (verse 10). This displayed Ruth's heart, a heart that appreciates kindness and the opportunity to serve. The foundation for a blessed marriage was born at this moment. Boaz complemented Ruth, and she rejoiced in his loving authority.

Boaz invited her to his table. Ruth ate and went back to the fields. When she finished, she took some grain to Naomi, and Naomi asked where she had gleaned. When Ruth told her she had gleaned with Boaz, Naomi said he was one of her closest relatives (verses17-20).

In chapter 3, Naomi told Ruth that Boaz is a kinsman and came up with a plan. She instructed Ruth to wash, anoint herself, put on her best clothes, and go down to the threshing floor where Boaz sleeps. Then Ruth was to uncover his feet while he was sleeping, lie down, and Boaz would tell her what to do (verses 2-5). Ruth obeyed as instructed and a beautiful relationship began.

When Boaz was resting, Ruth went and uncovered his feet to lie down. In the middle of the night, Boaz was startled and awoke to see a woman lying at his feet. He asked her name and she said, "I am Ruth your maid. So spread your covering over your maid, for you are a close relative" (verses 7-9, NASB).

Boaz said he would do whatever she asked, because Ruth was known as a "woman of excellence" in the city. He told her there was a closer relative than he, and if he did not redeem Ruth, then he would. So Ruth stayed at his feet until morning and rose early to not let anyone know she had been there (verses 10-14).

The beginning of chapter 4 shows that Boaz is determined to prove his love for Ruth. His goal was to make her his beautiful bride, so that he could cherish her for life and give her all that he had. He talked to "the closet relative of Naomi" and explained the situation regarding Ruth. They discussed the kinsman redeemer right concerning Ruth, and the kinsman redeemer right was given to Boaz (verses 1-10).

Boaz took Ruth for his wife, and she gave birth to a son who was named Obed. In time Obed fathered Jesse, and Jesse became the father of David (verses 13-22), who later became the anointed king of Israel (1 Samuel 16:1-13). For Ruth, it was a marvelous transition of renouncing her Moabite culture of many gods and receiving the culture of Israel's one God.

Ruth established herself as a name among great women of history. Ruth had a heart filled with wisdom and love, and will always be a great role model that empowers "holy" change resulting from faith in God.

In Hebrew, Ruth means "Friend." From Naomi's lifestyle, Ruth knew what the true God was like and wanted God as her friend, and He wanted her as His beloved to cherish. They both rejoiced in fellowship with each other. Ruth and Boaz are now in Heaven where all are cherished with eternal love.

Before leaving this story, there is some insight for us to consider. When Ruth slept at the feet of Boaz, this meant she submitted to his authority for leadership and protection. Proper spiritual leadership is a must for the husband. Having authority to lead a wife does not permit a husband to abuse his wife in any way. She is to be cherished with "love from Above."

Our revelation of cherished ladies will now turn to the New Testament. Mary, the mother of Jesus' human nature, is a blessed and remembered woman for all generations to come (Luke 1:46-49). Luke 1:26-38 gives clear information on the angel Gabriel's visit to Mary. Chapter 1 in Matthew's Gospel also sheds more insight about the virgin birth of Jesus, and that He will save His people from their sins (verses 18-24).

The prophet Isaiah foretold this miraculous virgin birth hundreds of years in advance and said this Person would be "God with us" (Isaiah 7:14). Some reject the possibility of the virgin birth. But "with God all things are possible" (Matthew 19:26). The Genesis account of creation cites that "from the dust of the ground, man was created." So, is it too difficult for the Almighty to make a woman conceive without intercourse to help humanity with love, grace, and forgiveness?

Mary was quite surprised when the angel appeared to her. As she listened to his words, she replied, "Let it be done according to your word" (Luke 1:38). Because she would be pregnant before her wedding day, she knew her people would think of her as a harlot and ostracize her. However, she bore the insults and trusted in the Word of the LORD, which was delivered by the angel. Strong women who stand by truth are a blessing to admire.

People have wondered how the traveling ministry of Jesus was supported. Luke 8:1-3 provides the answer. A reading of these verses shows that women of love and appreciation for Jesus, along with "many others," were public in supporting His Gospel of love and His twelve apostles. The "many others" would include men, for Jewish men supported God's work.

> [2]and also some women who had been healed of evil spirits and sicknesses: Mary who was called Magdalene, from whom seven demons had gone out, [3]and Joanna the wife of Chuza, Herod's steward, and Susanna, and many others who were contributing to their support out of their private means (NASB).

The names of these ladies were saved in Scripture to send us a message. Specifically, that the ladies are to be seen and remembered as very important in supporting the foundation of God's Gospel of love.

Mary Magdalene was very thankful and loyal to Jesus for casting seven demons out of her. Matthew 28:1 records that on the first day of the week, she and another Mary were the first to visit the tomb where Jesus had been buried after His crucifixion. But the tomb was empty. He had been raised physically from the dead as He foretold in John 2:19-21. Verses 2-10 in Matthew 28 mention their encounter with Jesus as they went to tell the apostles.

At first, some of the men did not believe the women's report, but Peter ran to the tomb for proof, looked inside the tomb, and it was empty (Luke 24:6-12). Isn't it amazing that the twelve apostles spent three years with Jesus, which was much more time than any woman spent with Him during His ministry, and they didn't fully understand His "prophetic resurrection words?"

Later the men believed, and all except John, were put to an early death, because they preached Christ's Gospel of love and forgiveness in various parts of the world (Acts 1:8). This Gospel message of equality (Galatians 3:27-28) was well received in the Roman Empire by women, because they had not been esteemed as highly as God had desired from the beginning of humanity.

Hebrews 11 gives recognition to men and women of great faith in serving God. This is a chapter that honors men and women of Old Testament history. They all had received "love from Above" and believed in His love to the point of giving their lives as proof.

Information in this chapter has established that God has always cherished women, and yes, He cherishes a relationship with men too. We must remember to cherish each other with "love from Above" on a daily basis. Reciprocating with kind words and deeds prove we cherish each other with His love. Let's make it our goal to cherish one another often. By doing this, we will be God's light that shines out in the darkness.

Like spring time flowers in full beauty bloom,
Precious women speak words filled with love.
Their heavenly, holy fragrance seeks a groom,
Bringing sweet honey lips on wings of a dove.

4

God Will Cherish
the Proverbs 31 Woman

The Book of Proverbs is packed with teachings of wisdom and warnings. King Solomon is the author, and sometimes he uses descriptions that are difficult to understand. However, this last section of Scripture in Proverbs 31:10-31 is presented in a way that is easy for all to understand and appreciate. I will group passages to focus our attention on the descriptions of a beautiful and amazing woman. Her traits emphasize the many qualities that are found in a precious woman of God.

Verses 10-12 will start our insight into a precious woman who glorifies God and cares for her family.

> [10]An excellent wife, who can find? For her worth is far above jewels.

> [11]The heart of her husband trusts in her, and he will have no lack of gain.

> [12]She does him good and not evil. All the days
> of her life.

Solomon begins his description of an excellent wife by saying such a woman is not an easy find. Then he declares her worth is "far above jewels." Because of her special heart, her husband trusts her and his gain is inevitable. Verse 12 is a captivating compliment about an excellent wife, for she "does her husband good, not evil, all the days of her life." A wife who is determined to do good all her life is a rare find.

In verses 13-15, we are shown that her eyes are set to find the needed items, and her hands are delighted to spend time shaping the needs. And she will bring food from afar to feed the family. Before the sun gives the morning light, she is up to prepare food for the household and maidens.

> [13]She looks for wool and flax, and works with
> her hands in delight.
>
> [14]She is like merchant ships; She brings her food
> from afar.
>
> [15]She rises also while it is still night, and gives
> food to her household and portions to her
> maidens.

Upon arising, the heart of this unique lady is warm with love before the sunrise warms the bodies of her family. Her planning and caring for her family is a wakeup blessing to all.

God Will Cherish the Proverbs 31 Woman

Because her husband trusts in her, she has the freedom to invest in a field and plants a vineyard that will provide food and income. She works in her investment field, and her arms are strong due to her persistent labor. Though she knows her gain is good, she continues to do what is needed at night as stated in the following verses 16-18.

> [16]She considers a field and buys it; From her earnings she plants a vineyard.
>
> [17]She girds herself with strength, and makes her arms strong.
>
> [18]She senses that her gain is good; Her lamp does not go out at night.

As we read verses 19-22, we find this lady of dignity does not limit her service to her family only. She helps the poor and needy, and her hands are once again busy. Snow does not concern her, for she has clothed her household in scarlet. Her clothing is fine linen and purple. She deserves this beauty.

> [19]She stretches out her hands to the distaff, and her hands grasp the spindle.
>
> [20]She extends her hand to the poor, and she stretches out her hands to the needy.
>
> [21]She is not afraid of the snow for her household, for all her household are clothed with scarlet.

[22]She makes coverings for herself; Her clothing
is fine linen and purple.

Verses 23-25 show the impact this holy woman has in her community. Her husband is a man of prestige and sits among men of stature. While he does what he should be doing, she continues on her journey of success by selling garments and belts. His wife is spiritually clothed with strength and dignity, and because of her disciplined lifestyle, she has a smiling outlook on life. She sees opportunity for more achievements.

[23]Her husband is known in the gates, when he
sits among the elders of the land.

[24]She makes linen garments and sells them, and
supplies belts to the tradesmen.

[25]Strength and dignity are her clothing, and she
smiles at the future.

Her virtues continue to be stated in verses 26-29. She speaks with wisdom and kindness and does not waste time being idle. She looks after her household, and her husband and children bless and praise her. He declares his wife excels all.

[26]She opens her mouth in wisdom, and the
teaching of kindness is on her tongue.

[27]She looks well to the ways of her household,
and does not eat the bread of idleness.

²⁸Her children rise up and bless her; Her husband also, and he praises her, saying:

²⁹"Many daughters have done nobly, but you excel them all."

The two final verses of God's description of a wonderful wife bring a warning and guidelines of freedom. She is not to focus on charm and beauty. Charm can manipulate for improper gain, and if beauty is emphasized above the heart of love, then pride can enter her life. When pride enters, the tendency to compare one's beauty against another will lead to bitterness or vanity.

Ladies who honor the LORD will show reverence for His ways of righteousness and be praised for their holy character. When a wife is not controlled by charm and beauty, she will keep her hands busy. This will increase her inner beauty. Her works will be known in the city, and she will be praised. Continue to allow her freedom to excel where she is gifted.

³⁰Charm is deceitful and beauty is vain, But a woman who fears the LORD, she shall be praised.

³¹ Give her the product of her hands, and let her works praise her in the gates (NASB).

We must remember that this information was written over 2,500 years ago. A wife's duties are no longer identical to the

Proverbs 31:10-31 list. However, there are some things that are evident, such as making the most of your time, taking care of basic family needs, and considering the poor.

What is important in any marriage is that the wife is given continued recognition and support from her husband and children. It is the husband's responsibility to make sure his wife is praised and blessed for all she does to help the family. If both are working, then discuss shared duties.

The numerous verses covered reveal that it is hard to find an excellent wife. But does the Bible have an area where certain verses tell a husband how he is to treat and honor his wife? We will now turn to some verses in the New Testament that shed more light on this question of ordained responsibility in marriage.

> [25]Husbands, love your wives, just as Christ also loved the church and gave Himself up for her, [26] so that He might sanctify her, having cleansed her by the washing of water with the word, [27] that He might present to Himself the church in all her glory, having no spot or wrinkle or any such thing; but that she would be holy and blameless. [28]So husbands ought also to love their own wives as their own bodies. He who loves his own wife loves himself; [29]for no one ever hated his own flesh, but nourishes and cherishes it, just as Christ also does the church (Ephesians 5:25-29, NASB).

Concerning the husband's responsibility to his wife, these verses are easy to understand. The husband's love for his wife should be a copy of Christ's love for His church of believers. The husband should love his wife so much that he would be willing to give his life for her.

The phrase "having cleansed her by the washing of the water with the word" refers to Bible verses read to her (John 15:3). Reading the Bible together allows the Holy Spirit to help you interact and communicate better. Also, the husband is to love (look after) his wife's own flesh as if it is his own. When this is done, it proves he cherishes her. When the husband follows these verses, his wife will submit alongside him to form a "love bond" of cooperation and help (Ephesians 5:22).

Husbands bow to propose, but do they maintain the same attitude of looking up to their beautiful bride who has blessed them with many of the qualities of the Proverbs 31 woman? When the proposal is made, you are telling your engaged princess that you want her to be your lifelong queen and you will cherish her consistently. Look up to her daily. Cherish and praise her, and she will submit to your Biblical wisdom and authoritative love that seeks to protect her in everything.

Make it a daily practice to cherish each other with words, gentle touches, and a countenance that shows approval. The word "caress" has a pretty definition. It means to "to touch or stroke tenderly or lovingly." Husbands and wives, please caress each other often and show fondness. Touch and stroke the heart, mind, and body with words of "love from Above."

Lifting a voice of praise, our hands will raise.
With verses of love, He sustains us for our days.
From our heart to our lips, His Spirit moves prayers.
To His throne words rise, as He blesses our verbal cares.

5

Prayer and Praise
Move Us to Cherish God

Prayer and praise to God are essential in achieving fulfillment in a spiritual journey that leads to authentic and everlasting love. This chapter will list numerous verses that show the different ways to offer prayer and praise to the One Who cherishes our words that come His way. You might be surprised to find out how easy it is to pray and to praise our God of love.

We will start with explaining the ways we can connect with God. For our convenience, the Bible mentions several options we can use to communicate with God. We are His beloved. Therefore, He has ordained various ways of verbal communication to accommodate all personalities. Prayer is the first way of communication with God we will explore.

The New Strong's Exhaustive Concordance of the Bible lists hundreds of verses where the words "pray," "prayed," "prayer," and "praying" are found in the Bible. These words convey a basic meaning that is easy to understand, and we get direct understanding of prayer from Jesus in what is called

"The Lord's Prayer." Some refer to this prayer as "The prayer for His disciples." Matthew 6:7-15 provides a foundational teaching for understanding prayer.

[7]But when ye pray, use not vain repetitions, as the heathen do: for they think that they shall be heard for their much speaking.

[8]Be not ye therefore like unto them: for your Father knoweth what things ye have need of, before ye ask him.

[9]After this manner therefore pray ye: Our Father which art in heaven, Hallowed be thy name.

[10]Thy kingdom come. Thy will be done in earth, as it is in heaven.

[11]Give us this day our daily bread.

[12]And forgive us our debts, as we forgive our debtors.

[13]And lead us not into temptation, but deliver us from evil: For thine is the kingdom, and the power, and the glory, forever. Amen.

[14]For if ye forgive men their trespasses, your heavenly Father will also forgive you:

[15]But if ye forgive not men their trespasses, neither will your Father forgive your trespasses (KJV).

Prayer and Praise Move Us to Cherish God

It would take pages to explain this prayer teaching in an expository manner, so I will briefly share the content. Don't be repetitive (vain repetitions, mantras, chanting) to be heard for your words (verse 7), and don't act like people who do this (verse 8). Verse 9 tells us we are praying to our heavenly Father, and His Name is holy so present your words as holy unto Him.

We are to pray that His will be done on earth, because He knows the needs of people. We are used to accomplish His will, which portrays a Kingdom that gives a glimpse of what Heaven is like (verse 10). Daily food is requested, and this includes sharing with your neighbor (verse 11). Keep in mind this teaching is in the plural ("our").

Verse 12 says, as God forgives our debts (moral and spiritual debts to God), we are to forgive our debtors. This precedes a very revealing verse 13, which is a plea. The proper translation for "lead us not into temptation" is "do not allow us to be led into temptation."[1] We are asking God to deliver (protect) us from evil or "the evil one" that leads us into sin.

A vital conditional statement is found in verse 14. The word "if" warns us that forgiveness is a must. Yet, "if" we do not forgive those who trespass (offend us or fall away from the truth) against us, our heavenly Father will not forgive us for our trespasses (verse 15).

If we do not forgive those who hurt us, we become bitter and angry. Not forgiving eats up the peace and health we need. Often, those who do not forgive, suffer more anguish than the ones who committed the wrong.

This prayer is spoken worldwide by individuals and congregations, because it reveals various requests we can present before God that reveal His will. Thus, it is clear that "prayer is talking to God" about concerns and needs. This prayer was taught early in Christ's ministry. Let's look at a prayer that He prayed during the last week of His ministry, before He was crucified.

Chapter 17 of John's Gospel contains 26 verses. This prayer shows how much Jesus loved His disciples, as well as those who would later believe in Him and follow His teachings. Rather than print all 26 verses, teachings from specific verses in this chapter will be presented.

> Verse 1. Jesus begins by saying the hour (time) has come to glorify the Son of God.

> Verses 2-3. Eternal life is found in knowing the only true God *and* Jesus Christ. With these words, Jesus claims to be Israel's Messiah.

> Verses 4-5. Jesus mentions He had glory with His Father before the world was. This means Jesus took part in creating the world (Genesis 1:1). See John 1:1-3 and Colossians 1:16-17.

> Verses 6-8. The Father's Name and words to be spoken by Jesus were established.

> Verses 13-16. He desires that His words bring joy to His followers, and they need to be aware that they will be hated by some people.

Verses 17-19. These are very powerful verses, because Jesus says "His Father's word is truth." Sanctify means to make holy and separate or set apart God's people for purity to represent the One Who sanctifies them.

Verses 20-26. Jesus prays for those in the future (that's us) who will believe in him and His words of truth, to be with Him in heavenly glory, and be one in unity of love.

These two prayers are excellent examples of teaching people how to pray and present concerns before God. Prayer is simply talking to God and asking or pleading with Him for certain things. Such requests can be for others or ourselves. Anyone who takes time to read the Bible will find that Scriptures are saturated with the words "pray," "prayed," "prayer," and "prayers." And there is a reason for this. He wants to hear from us to let us know He is a God Who desires a personal relationship with us.

There are other historical instances that encourage us to verbally communicate with our Creator. Let's look at these, and see what they reveal about talking to God. The phrase "call upon" has a strong meaning. It is first used in Genesis 4:26 to describe men beginning to "call upon" the Name of the LORD. They were acknowledging His sovereign Name, appealing to Him, and seeking His help.

Other Scriptural records of people calling upon the LORD are found in Deuteronomy 4:7, 1 Chronicles 16:8, Psalm 18:3,

55:16, 80:18, 86:5-7, 99:6, and Romans 10:12-14. When reading through these verses, it is clear that those "calling upon" God believed He would answer in time.

The word "ask" is used often in the Bible. It is another way to verbally approach God. Scriptural examples of "ask" are found in Isaiah 45:11, Matthew 7:7, Ephesians 3:20, James 1:5-6, 4:2-3, and 1 John 3:22; 5:14-15.

A common teaching that encourages us to ask God for His supernatural help is found in John 14:13-14. Jesus tells us to ask anything in His Name, and He will do it. The phrase "in My Name" means anything within the will of His Name. So when we present our words before God, we should consider "the will" of our motives.

Philippians 4:6-7 are verses many have memorized for guidance and prayer strength in life. They read:

> [6]Be anxious for nothing, but in everything by prayer and supplication with thanksgiving let your requests be made known to God.

> [7]And the peace of God, which surpasses all comprehension, will guard your hearts and your minds in Christ Jesus (NASB).

The word "supplication" in verse 6 represents a verbal petition for favor or mercy. It is a strong appeal to God that can accompany prayer. In Hebrews 5:7, we are given a classic look at the prayer life of Jesus. "Prayers and supplications" were offered up while He was on the earth.

Prayer and Praise Move Us to Cherish God

Our prayer journey has established that there is more than one way to approach God. I've used all of these many times in my 46 years as a Christian. Situations fluctuate and so do our ways of appeal for God's help.

One thing I have noticed, while reading through the entire New Testament, Jesus and His apostles never taught any type of prayer to angels, deceased relatives, or prominent historical spiritual people. Our heavenly prayer fellowship is with the Father and His Son only (1 John 1:3).

What the Bible teaches about prayer gives us the opportunity to cherish God as our friend and have Him cherish back with answering our prayers. An authentic spiritual love journey through prayer is God's desire for all. We are His beloved, and we are precious treasures to Him.

Always remember that God answers prayers according to His will (1 John 5:14-15). Also, husbands who don't honor their wives properly (1 Peter 3:7) should not expect a clear path to God's throne of grace for answers (Hebrews 4:16).

We will now move into the subject of praise, which is an area of humility, excitement, recognition of God, people, and accomplishments.

Like prayer, praise is an essential way of communicating with God. Praise is important, because it is mentioned over 200 times in the Bible. By definition, praise can mean "to celebrate, commend, glory, sing about God, or boast about God."[2] Praise expresses our approval of God for Who He is and what He does, but people can also be praised for their appearance (Genesis 12:15) or works.

Numerous examples of praise will be listed to show the importance of this activity for cherishing the true God of love, for He rules with "love from Above." We will see how He cherishes us as we praise Him in many ways. It will be evident that compliments are a part of praise, and everyone likes and deserves compliments.

With hundreds of verses describing praise, it would be helpful to cite some ways the Bible displays them. Singing praises about God and His Name is found in these Scriptures:

> Judges 5:3; 2 Chronicles 20:22; 29:30; Ezra 3:10-11; Nehemiah 12:46; Psalm 9:2; 18:49; 21:13; 27:6; 28:7; 30:12; 47:6; 57:7; 61:8; 68:4; 75:9; 92:1; 98:4; 104:33; 106:12; 108:1; 135:3; 138:1; 144:9; 146:2; 147:1, 7; 149:3; Jeremiah 20:13; Acts 16:25; Hebrews 2:12.

Throughout history, these numerous verses have taught the ongoing joy of singing praises to God and His Name of unique identity. Musical instruments also impact the praise given to God, so let's list some Bible verses that reveal instruments of praise:

> Ezra 3:10 (trumpets and cymbals); Psalm 43:4, 144:9 (harp) and 147:7 (lyre); 149:3 (timbrel, harp); 150:3-5 (trumpet, harp, lyre, timbrel, stringed instruments, loud cymbals).

Prayer and Praise Move Us to Cherish God

Singing and musical instruments are connected to praise. We can't all play instruments to praise God, but we can use our mouth as an instrument of praise. The mouth is the best instrument of praise, because it's always with us.

When realizing there are over 200 references to praise in the Bible, we have covered only a small amount of them, but it has given us a clear understanding of the importance of praise to God. Should you continue to read through the many praise verses found in the Bible, you will see that praise unto God was and is a way of life to cherish Him for His continuous blessings. In response, He will prove He cherishes us with answered prayers and activating joy in us.

Psalm 22:3 says "the Lord inhabits the praises of Israel" (KJV). When this was written, Israel was the only nation worshipping the true God. Since that time, the nations of the world have been given the opportunity through the New Covenant (New Testament) to receive God's forgiveness of their sins, and for their praises to be inhabited by the Lord of love.

We are His beloved. He holds us dear in His thoughts, treats us tenderly with care and affection, and keeps us secure as a priority to cherish. Our thoughts are precious to Him. They allow our God to prepare blessings in advance and when they arrive, it is common for us to offer up joyous praise to Him.

Hebrews 13:15 reminds us to "offer up the sacrifice of praise to God continually, that is, the fruit of our lips giving thanks to His Name" (KJV). Praise and thanks are linked with love and bring joy and peace to our inner being.

The first century believers in Jesus made it a lifestyle to incorporate praise in multiple ways as recorded in Colossians 3:16, which reads:

> Let the word of Christ dwell in you richly in all wisdom; teaching and admonishing one another in psalms, and hymns, and spiritual songs, singing with grace in your hearts to the Lord (KJV).

Though the word "praise" is not mentioned in this verse, what is presented is instruction for living a victorious life that can handle all circumstances. This verse indicates that the hearts of Christians were blessing each other in several ways in the midst of a cruel and brutal Roman Empire. The singing of spiritual songs in hearts to the Lord was praise for His grace and forgiveness freely given to all who wanted it.

The Scriptures teach that music is connected to praise. It revives us. Praise releases the Holy Spirit in us to increase His strength, confidence, and peace within us. The joy of the LORD is our strength. When we praise Him, His joy circulates through our entire being. Praise is water for a thirsty soul. Praise is a release of bound up emotions by acknowledging someone or God in a joyous, complimentary, or respectful manner.

Countless praises have been offered to God in music for thousands of years. Millions of praises to Him, His works, and His holy Name go forth daily. As we look around, we see the glory of His creation, and with awe we praise Him with a variety of words and emotional expressions, sometimes not even realizing we are praising the LORD of creation. Ultimately, prayer and praise lead to continual thanksgiving as found in 1 Thessalonians 5:16-18, which reads:

> [16]Rejoice evermore. [17]Pray without ceasing. [18]In everything give thanks: for this is the will of God in Christ Jesus concerning you (KJV).

A life that combines prayer, praise, and giving thanks is a life that will overcome adversity and shine like a light in any darkness. Such a life is cherished and supported by God. Being created in His spiritual image opens up a reciprocating Holy Spirit relationship composed of prayer, praise, rejoicing, and thanksgiving that brings His blessings.

Endnote:

1. A. T. Robertson, *Word Pictures in the New Testament, Gospels According to Matthew and Mark, Volume I* (Nashville, Tennessee, Broadman Press, 1930), p. 54.

2. W. E. Vine, Merrill F. Unger, William White, Jr. *Vine's Complete Expository Dictionary of Old and New Testament Words* (Nashville, Tennessee, Thomas Nelson Publishers, 1985), pp. 184-185, Hebrew word section, pp. 479-480, Greek word section.

Love nailed to a cross removes all barriers.
Those believing this are cherished love carriers.
God's ambassador servants will teach all to caress.
For the joy of His love will always be theirs to possess.

6

Blessed Are Those
Who Cherish With Love

To have a broader understanding of explaining how God wants His people to be known as those who cherish people, the details are found in 1 Corinthians 13:1-13. These Scriptures give numerous teachings on how we can role model "cherish" in everyday life. This chapter is often read through at weddings, and on occasions the groom and bride will quote specific verses to each other from memory.

In chapter 12, the apostle Paul explains that God gives different gifts, ministries, and spiritual manifestations of the Holy Spirit gifts to individuals (verses 4-11). Each spiritual gift is to be viewed as important and needed. The gifts are not for individual superiority, but for the common good in service to help others and give recognition to God.

Apparently, some had become arrogant about the gift they received, believing some gifts were more important than others. This attitude belittled the work and will of the Holy Spirit. So Paul took time to use the human body as an example of all parts being important and needed for proper functioning (verses 12-31). After this correction was written, Paul captured their focus by stating the most meaningful, powerful, and heart-changing love scenario for character development. There is much to learn, verse by verse, from what many have called "the love chapter of the Bible" or "God's definition of love."

> [1]If I speak with the tongues of men and of angels, but do not have love, I have become a noisy gong or a clanging cymbal.

The Christians at Corinth, Greece, were placing too much importance on the gift of tongues of men and angels. Those possessing the gift of tongues were filled with the Holy Spirit at times to speak in a language they had never been taught. Paul says that if they have this gift but do not have love, they are just making words of noise.

> [2]If I have the gift of prophecy, and know all mysteries and all knowledge; and if I have all faith, so as to remove mountains, but do not have love, I am nothing.

More supernatural gifts are mentioned by Paul in this verse; gifts of powerful faith, prophecy, insight to mysteries, and all knowledge. He concludes by saying that if a person possesses any of these gifts and does not have love (true love from God), such a person is nothing.

Blessed Are Those Who Cherish With Love

³And if I give all my possessions to feed the
poor, and if I surrender my body to be burned,
but do not have love, it profits me nothing.

The issues of generosity and self-sacrifice are listed. If a
person gives in these ways, and does not do it out of love, but
does it to be noticed, there is no profit before God in it.

⁴Love is patient, love is kind and is not jealous;
love does not brag and is not arrogant,

After telling us what love is not about, this devoted
servant of God begins telling us what truly describes love in
verse 4. Love is an attribute of God (1 John 4:9, 11, 16).
Therefore, we should remember that the word used for "love"
in this chapter refers to God's love. There are other Greek
words for "love" that convey a "friendly" or "brotherly" love,
but Paul does not use them in this chapter. His purpose is to
teach us to display behavior with love as representatives of the
Almighty God.

God's patience with people is found in 2 Peter 3:9 where
it says, "He is patient, not wishing for any to perish without
eternal life, but for all to come to repentance." That type of
patience should be applied to all situations when working with
various persons. Our love attitude should be shown with verbal
and physical kindness. Being jealous of what others have is not
to be a part of our love for others. We are all gifted and blessed
in different ways. Our God is a God of diversity.

Bragging about our accomplishments goes against complimenting the achievements of others, and it sets up a blockade for humility. Possessing an arrogant disposition does not allow for correction and looks down on struggling people.

> [5]does not act unbecomingly; it does not seek its
> own, is not provoked, does not take into account
> a wrong suffered,

One who is "becoming" portrays a suitable or attractive presence. "Unbecoming" is the opposite. It displays a presence that is not suitable or attractive for the circumstance at hand. When in doubt, be silent. God's love does not seek its own welfare. Rather, it seeks to further the well-being of those who need help.

To provoke someone is to incite them to anger. This is easy to do when discussing and disagreeing about an issue. An atmosphere of patience, kindness, and verbal gentleness is essential when dealing with differing views in an attempt to see the right view.

This next love component, when not followed properly, has led to severed friendships and divorces. If we do not forgive those who have wronged us (sinned against us) and keep a mental list against them, the inner grudge we retain does not allow for the relationship to be healed. It will be impossible for the once uplifting relationship we had to be pleasant, as it once was. When we see that person or hear their name, we will be defensive rather than forgiving.

⁶does not rejoice in unrighteousness, but rejoices with the truth;

Love does not rejoice in being a part of or participating in wicked and sinful conduct. Love rejoices when the truth is revealed so that repentance can transpire. Also, when the truth is showcased, it leads more people to righteousness.

⁷bears all things, believes all things, hopes all things, endures all things.

We all go through tough, painful, and disappointing times during our lifetime. We have to persevere, bear each other's burdens, and believe for the best outcome in all things. Hope is essential. Jesus is our blessed hope, and the Holy Spirit intercedes for us (Romans 8:26) so that we can have spiritual endurance.

⁸Love never fails; but if there are gifts of prophecy, they will be done away; if there are tongues, they will cease; if there is knowledge, it will be done away.

Now we are told that love never fails, but what does this mean? It means that persistent and enduring love never fails to please God, and it builds us to represent His nature of love. Holy Spirit gifts that were mentioned at the first part of the chapter will pass away when no longer needed, but not love.

[9]For we know in part and we prophesy in part;

Partial knowledge and partial prophecy will guide us for a time as needed, but verse 10 teaches us that there is a time when these gifts will not be needed.

[10]but when the perfect comes, the partial will be done away.

Much discussion has taken place over the words "when the perfect comes" and what they represent. Some believe it refers to the completion of the books in the Bible. Others believe it has a direct connection to Jesus, the perfect One, coming back down from Heaven to rule on earth in the future. And some believe the words refer to when we are in Heaven where all is perfect. Whatever is correct, why not rejoice in the "perfect inspiration of the Bible" (2 Timothy 3:16), and the fact that the Bible records that Jesus, the "perfect One," will come again to the earth (Acts 1:11).

[11]When I was a child, I used to speak like a child, think like a child, reason like a child; when I became a man, I did away with childish things.

This verse is pleasant. Paul tells the Christians that it's not proper to be like a child who doesn't really have a deep reasoning and understanding of love. They are to grow up in

Blessed Are Those Who Cherish With Love

God's love for each other by practicing the previous love guidelines.

> [12]For now we see in a mirror dimly, but then face to face; now I know in part, but then I will know fully just as I also have been fully known.

This brilliant and great apostle states in a humble manner that we don't have a clear understanding of every subject. Thus, if we live in love for one another, then God's love is seen and copied, and explosive disagreements are rare.

> [13]But now abide faith, hope, love, these three; but the greatest of these is love (NASB).

As this Bible chapter comes to an end, we are told that faith, hope, and love are to abide in us. But the greatest character trait a person can have is God's love, which was covered in the previous 12 verses. Our world needs a constant overflowing, daily dose of God's love. Are you going to help the world be more pleasant with love from Above?

The word for God's love (*agapē*) is used numerous times in the New Testament, and there is a purpose. While on earth, Jesus always modeled "love from Above." In John 13:34-35, He commands His disciples to love one another, and by this all people will know they are His disciples.

God's love is expressed as available for all in John 3:16 where it says, "For God so loved the world (all the people) that

He gave His only begotten Son, that whoever believes in Him will not perish (when he dies), but will have eternal life (with God forever). To emphasize God's love, Jesus taught that He causes the sun and rain to fall upon all people (Matthew 5:45) and is kind to ungrateful and evil people (Luke 6:35).

Sometimes, genuine love that proceeds from God's nature is not lived out consistently among those who call themselves Christians. This has become a stumbling block in persuading people to embrace the everlasting love and forgiveness that Jesus gives freely to anyone at any time.

No one is perfect, but those who claim to be followers of and believers in Jesus Christ should consider memorizing 1 Corinthians 13:4-8. I quote this passage daily as a reminder to think and act in a loving manner and to grow more in God's love, as presented in this chapter. Yes, I still have room for improvement.

Love can be a verb showing active involvement or a noun that describes its qualities. Both the noun and the verb combine to fulfill the complete definition of love. To be effective, love must be active. The various Greek words that define God's love, brotherly love, or friendly love, are found hundreds of times in the Bible. That should send a message to us that we are commanded to love God and one another constantly.

We are God's beloved, created in His image to be like Him. Our spiritual journey guides us to love people according to 1 Corinthians 13. Along the daily way, we remember to cherish (hold dear, treat tenderly with care and affection, keep in mind, cling to in thought) with words and smiles.

Also, we can apply another layer of love by using discretion when caressing (touching, stroking tenderly, or lovingly) someone. These two "C words," cherish and caress, must be our identity, proving we are heavenly vessels of love that change lives around the world.

Over 35 years ago, while in prayer, I asked the LORD for a spiritual ministry of love, wisdom, and truth. The wisdom and truth came quickly, and I enjoyed having His wisdom and truth for guidance and helping others. Yet along the way, I was hurt repeatedly and that blocked the most vital part of my prayer request, which was to have a ministry of love to all people.

In the last 5 years, my life has changed. I have surrendered my will that was protecting my hurts, yet blocking the fullness of God's love, in exchange for His will to heal my broken heart with divine love. "Healing the broken-hearted" is the heart and will of Jesus' ministry as recorded in Luke 4:18 (KJV). I am now learning to cherish people with His love.

All people are precious treasure chests waiting to be unlocked for a lifetime of joy and happiness. God's love from each heart does the unlocking and the healing. We have looked at His love guideline in this chapter. Let's follow it forever and if we do, there will be less spiritual and material poverty in our world, as exemplified in the next chapter.

God's love and mercy are waiting to be shown.
Everywhere are those in need who hurt and moan.
Our selfish pace in life chooses to eliminate caring.
It's time that other people's burdens we begin bearing.

7

Good Samaritans
Cherish All People

Many have heard the phrase "the Good Samaritan." What does this mean, and where can we find its origin? Before this question is answered, we need accurate history of the Samaritan people. For this information, the Old Testament provides our answers. Samaria is located north of Jerusalem.

The content of 2 Kings 17:29 tells us about the culture of the people in the land of Samaria. It reads:

> But every nation still made gods of its own and
> put them in the houses of the high places which
> the people of Samaria had made, every nation in
> which their cities they lived (NASB).

Unlike the wandering Israelites, who worshipped one God (monotheism), the people in this area were polytheistic and worshipped many gods. Their demonic worship and choices of sacrifices to their gods were an abomination to Israel's God.

Thus, the God of Israel did not want His people to intermarry with the Samaritans. The exception to this was if the Samaritan renounced the worship of idols and gods and received the God of Israel to worship. Then the spiritually converted Samaritan was accepted as a worshipper of the true God of Israel.

Look back at the story of Ruth and Boaz in chapter 3. Ruth renounced her god and received the God Boaz worshipped and followed. This made her spiritually acceptable to the Almighty God, and proof of this was her allegiance to Him.

But if an Israelite married a Samaritan or any Gentile that did not renounce idol worship and gods that were against the God of Israel, they were called spiritual dogs (half-breeds), as recorded in Matthew 15:26. In this setting, Jesus cast a demon out of the daughter of a Canaanite woman after she pleads with Him for help.

The New Testament sheds more insight concerning the Samaritans to let us know how God has reached out to cherish them with love. At the right time, they played a part in spreading God's message of love to the nations. In Matthew 10:5-6, Jesus tells His disciples "to not enter any cities of the Gentiles or Samaritans, but to go to the lost sheep of Israel." Jesus was sent first to Israel to strengthen them to proclaim His message of forgiveness for all sins.

In Luke 9:52-53, Jesus was going to enter a Samaritan village, but they would not receive Him. Two of His disciples wanted to command fire from Heaven to consume those who had rejected Jesus. How did Jesus respond? He rebuked them for their hostile spiritual attitude. Then He referred to Himself as "the Son of Man who did not come to destroy lives, but to save them" (verse 54-56). God is patient with those who reject Him, for He is love (1 John 4:8, 11, 16).

The Gospels record that healing various diseases was a common part of Christ's ministry. Luke 17:11-19 describes His healing of 10 lepers. Lepers were kept away from the population for fear of transmitting the disease. When the 10 were healed, they began going back to town. One of them turned back, glorifying God with a loud voice. He fell on his face at the feet of Jesus, giving thanks. He was a Samaritan.

Chapter 4 of John's Gospel presents a situation where Jesus encountered a Samaritan woman while passing through the city of Sychar in Samaria. Jesus was weary from His journey and stopped by Jacob's well for water (verses 4-6). A Samaritan woman came to draw water, and Jesus asked her to give Him a drink. The woman recognized Jesus as a Jew and said, "How is it that you as a Jew ask me for a drink since I am a Samaritan woman?" She said this because Jews had no dealings with Samaritans (verse 9).

Jesus spent time telling her about the water He gives freely. Those who receive it will have "a well of water within that springs up to eternal life." The lady asked for this water (verses 14-15). As the dialogue continued, Jesus revealed details about her personal life. This lady is wise and responded by saying that He was a prophet (verses 16-19). Jesus continued talking to her and said "the Father is looking for those who will worship Him in spirit and truth" (verses 21-24).

The woman told Jesus that she knew "the Messiah (Christ) is coming and He will declare all things to us." Jesus told her He was that Person (verses 25-26). The woman left the well and went back into the city and told the men about Jesus, and they came out to see Him (verses 28-30).

Because of the encounter with the woman at Jacob's well, many Samaritans believed in Jesus as the Savior of the world (verses 39-42). Jesus only did as directed by His Father, and early in His three-year ministry He focused His time on the house of Israel. In this situation, He was sovereignly directed to this well to reach out to people who had been labeled as "spiritual dogs." God's love plan of forgiveness would cherish those, who for centuries, had rejected Him and His holy ways. He had not forgotten them. Through His Son, Jesus, He personally approached the Samaritans with "love from Above."

Another well-known teaching that involves a Samaritan deserves our attention. The story is recorded in Luke 10:30-37. This teaching will show us how to respond to people in need, because the world needs many who respond with mercy.

Luke 10:25 tells us a lawyer asked Jesus, "What must be done to inherit eternal life?" Jesus asked him, "What is written in the Law?" (verse 26). The lawyer said that a person must love the LORD God with all your heart and your neighbor as yourself (verse 27). Jesus commended his response and told the lawyer, "Do this and you will live" (verse 28).

However, this was not enough information for the lawyer, so he asked, "And who is my neighbor?" This is where the story (parable) of the Good Samaritan begins, a story that would have worldwide impact forever, because it tells us to love the needy we encounter as our neighbor. Let's learn about how to cherish people with "love from Above" from the One Who came from Heaven.

> [30]Jesus replied and said, "A man was going down from Jerusalem to Jericho, and fell among robbers, and they stripped him and beat him, and went away leaving him half dead.
>
> [31]"And by chance a priest was going down on that road, and when he saw him, he passed by on the other side.

Robbers stripped and beat a man, leaving him half dead. A priest saw the helpless man and did nothing to help him. He left the beaten man to make it on his own. Priests should be examples of compassion and oversee the immediate needs of people. Some priests like the position for prestige.

> [32] "Likewise a Levite also, when he came to the place and saw him, passed by on the other side.

Levites were trained to work in the Temple and were exposed to the sacred teachings of the LORD. They knew what God required for those in need. Yet, like the priest, the Levite ignored the physical needs of this beaten man. What caused these two men to walk away from a man in desperate need?

The phrase "on the other side" reveals our answer. The priest and Levite made an effort to put distance between the beaten man, who was a stranger to them. Most likely they did not want to take the time to touch a stranger and violate ceremonial contamination of the Law.[1] But Jesus, Who knew the Law well, was using this illustration to show the world about a new Law that would soon go into effect, the Law of Love for fellow man that all were to follow.

> [33]"But a Samaritan, who was on a journey, came upon him; and when he saw him, he felt compassion,
>
> [34]and came to him and bandaged up his wounds, pouring oil and wine on them; and he put him on his own beast, and brought him to an inn and took care of him.
>
> [35]"On the next day he took out two denarii and gave them to the innkeeper and said, 'Take care of him; and whatever more you spend, when I return I will repay you.'

Read through these three verses again to grasp the vast difference of mercy between the priest, Levite, and Samaritan. Remember, at this time, Samaritans were known as traitors to the Law and were given the title of "spiritual dogs," because they married those who were not of the Jewish faith. But how does Jesus present the Samaritan?

Good Samaritans Cherish All People

These next two verses provide our answer and we are given "a Jesus mandate" for all humanity to follow daily.

> [36]"Which of these three do you think proved to be a neighbor to the man who fell into the robbers' hands?"
>
> [37]And he said, "The one who showed mercy toward him." Then Jesus said to him, "Go and do the same" (NASB).

After His presentation of how mercy should be shown, Jesus put response pressure on the lawyer by asking him to say which of the three men proved to be a neighbor and showed mercy. He responded, and Jesus told the man to "Go and do the same." As opportunities come our way to love our fellow man as our neighbor, we must respond as the Samaritan did.

Jesus said He was the good Shepherd (John 10:14), and those who follow Him are His sheep. Thus, they display His teaching of good works, and are known for their acts of mercy that help neighbors in need. By using the Samaritan as an example of mercy, Jesus was foretelling how God would send us to cherish all people by caring for them with His love. This teaching has motivated many to help people worldwide.

Endnote:

1. A. T. Robertson, *Word Pictures in the New Testament, Volume II, The Gospel According to Luke* (Nashville, Tennessee, Broadman Press, 1930), p. 153.

A king with abundant wealth finds his bride.
His words and eyes have nothing to hide.
Her joyful response opens a passionate heart.
Their romance will flow with a holy start.

8

The Song of Songs
Sings "Cherish" in Marriage

Solomon was the son of King David (2 Samuel 12:24) and was the King of Israel for 40 years (1 Kings 11:42) after his father died. He wrote *Ecclesiastes* and the majority of *The Book of Proverbs*. Also, he wrote a controversial book titled *The Song of Songs*. This is the book that will receive our attention in this chapter. In this epic love poem, we find some explicit teachings and descriptions of love between a husband, King Solomon, and his Shulamite bride.

Before we move into the holy love that is found in this "song of romance," we need to point out that Solomon had a unique relationship with the LORD. We find in 1 Kings 3:5 that "the LORD appeared to Solomon in a dream by night." God told Solomon he could ask for what he wanted. Solomon asked for wisdom to understand the people and discern between good and bad (verse 8-9).

In 2 Timothy 3:16, it mentions that "all Scripture is inspired (God-breathed upon the mind of man) by God." When Paul wrote this, he was also referring to the Old Testament

Scriptures. Therefore, Solomon's inspired writings are the result of the leading of God's Holy Spirit. When you read some love-filled "inspired Scriptures" in this chapter, don't be surprised at the content. This book will show the love God wants for a husband and wife to share and enjoy to the utmost.

King Solomon spoke 3,000 proverbs and composed 1,005 songs (1 Kings 4:32). Clearly, God gave him abundant wisdom. Scholars disagree whether this love song is literal, allegorical, symbolical, or portrays combinations. One thing is evident after reading it carefully. It is written in a love song manner, abounding in metaphors and oriental imagery. The verses flow beautifully in expressing mutual love.

In some verses, I will put certain words in parenthesis to give more clarity to the meaning. The first verse of this book of romance informs us that this is "The song of songs, which is Solomon's" (KJV). And as we proceed to verse 2, you will read about two people who truly "cherish" each other.

> [2]Let him kiss me with the kisses of his mouth: for thy love is better than wine.

> [3]Because of the savour (fragrance) of thy good ointments thy name is as ointment poured forth, therefore do the virgins love thee.

> [4]Draw me, we will run after thee: the king hath brought me into his chambers: we will be glad and rejoice in thee, we will remember thy love more than wine: the upright love thee.

[5]I am black (dark), but comely (lovely), O ye daughters of Jerusalem, as the tents of Kedar, as the curtains of Solomon.

[6]Look not upon me, because I am black (dark), because the sun hath looked upon me: my mother's children were angry with me; they made me the keeper of the vineyards; but mine own vineyard have I not kept.

[7]Tell me, O thou whom my soul loveth, where thou feedest, where thou makest thy flock to rest at noon: for why should I be as one that turneth aside by the flocks of thy companions?

[8]If thou know not, O thou fairest among women, go thy way forth by the footsteps of the flock, and feed thy kids beside the shepherds' tents.

[9]I have compared thee, O my love, to a company of horses in Pharaoh's chariots.

[10]Thy cheeks are comely (lovely) with rows of jewels, thy neck with chains of gold.

[11]We will make thee borders of gold with studs of silver.

[12]While the king sitteth at his table, my spikenard sendeth forth the smell thereof.

[13]A bundle of myrrh is my well-beloved unto me; he shall lie all night between my breasts.

[14]My beloved is unto me as a cluster of camphire (henna blooms) in the vineyards of Engedi.

[15]Behold, thou art fair, my love; behold, thou art fair; thou hast doves' eyes.

[16]Behold, thou art fair, my beloved, yea, pleasant: also our bed is green.

[17]The beams of our house are cedar, and our rafters of fir.

The various descriptive words Solomon uses in this chapter show he wants to acknowledge the attractive aspects of this special woman, and she also sees him as appealing. Kisses with love better than wine (verse 2), her lovely cheeks and neck (verse10), spikenard perfume (verse 12), her well-beloved lying between her breasts all night (verse 13), a cluster of fragrance (verse 14), the gentle picture of doves' eyes (verse 15), and their bed is mentioned (verse 16).

This is romance, inspired and approved by God, which is precious in His sight. God is the Creator of the bonded love between a husband and wife. He leaves it up to them to magnify their love for each other as time goes on. Their bed (verse 16) is for them only.

Chapter 2

[1]I am the rose of Sharon, and the lily of the valleys.

[2]As the lily among thorns, so is my love among the daughters.

[3]As the apple tree among the trees of the wood, so is my beloved among the sons. I sat down under his shadow with great delight, and his fruit was sweet to my taste.

[4]He brought me to the banqueting house, and his banner over me was love.

[5]Stay me with flagons, comfort me with apples: for I am sick of love.

[6]His left hand is under my head, and his right hand doth embrace me.

[7]I charge you, O ye daughters of Jerusalem, by the roes, and by the hinds of the field, that ye stir not up, nor awake my love, till he please.

[8]The voice of my beloved! behold, he cometh leaping upon the mountains, skipping upon the hills.

[9] My beloved is like a roe (Gazelle) or a young hart (stag or male deer): behold, he standeth behind our wall, he looketh forth at the windows, shewing himself through the lattice.

[10]My beloved spake, and said unto me, Rise up, my love, my fair one, and come away.

[11]For, lo, the winter is past, the rain is over and gone;

[12]The flowers appear on the earth; the time of the singing of birds is come, and the voice of the turtle is heard in our land;

[13]The fig tree putteth forth her green figs, and the vines with the tender grape give a good smell. Arise, my love, my fair one, and come away.

[14]O my dove, that art in the clefts of the rock, in the secret places of the stairs, let me see thy countenance, let me hear thy voice; for sweet is thy voice, and thy countenance is comely.

[15]Take us the foxes, the little foxes that spoil the vines: for our vines have tender grapes.

[16]My beloved is mine, and I am his: he feedeth among the lilies.

[17]Until the day break, and the shadows flee away, turn, my beloved, and be thou like a roe or a young hart upon the mountains of Bether.

Chapter 2 begins with the portrait of beautiful flowers, the Rose of Sharon and the Lily. The coastal Plain of Sharon extends for several miles in Israel and has many flowers. The Rose of Sharon is a robust rose. I have one in my front yard that is 10 feet tall. It produces dozens of pink blossoms every year. The frost and 100 degree weather have not killed it in 17 years. It is beautiful and resistant to harsh conditions.

The two flowers presented speak of the woman's beauty and her strength in harsh situations. Solomon knows his "dark beauty of love," described in verses 5 and 6 in chapter 1, is a unique woman who sparkles with complete beauty.

She goes to his banqueting house (verse 4) and says these special words; "His banner over me was love." How precious. Because he treats her with "love from Above," her words display a treasure of appreciation from her heart. Verse 6 is a love description in itself, so I will make no comment except that those with holy love should embrace with agreement.

Verses 8-10 find her delighting in the sound of his voice, and he requests that she come with him. The springtime description of flowers, singing birds, and tasty crops come forth for both to enjoy (verses 11-13). She is his darling dove with a sweet voice and comely (attractive) countenance (verse 14). Verses 15 and 16 convey love and strength in their close relationship. In this chapter, both are given the lead in expressing their love. This is proper in a holy romance.

Chapter 3

¹By night on my bed I sought him whom my soul loveth: I sought him, but I found him not.

²I will rise now, and go about the city in the streets, and in the broad ways I will seek him whom my soul loveth: I sought him, but I found him not.

³The watchmen that go about the city found me: to whom I said, Saw ye him whom my soul loveth?

⁴It was but a little that I passed from them, but I found him whom my soul loveth: I held him, and would not let him go, until I had brought him into my mother's house, and into the chamber of her that conceived me.

⁵I charge you, O ye daughters of Jerusalem, by the roes, and by the hinds of the field, that ye stir not up, nor awake my love, till he please.

⁶Who is this that cometh out of the wilderness like pillars of smoke, perfumed with myrrh and frankincense, with all powders of the merchant?

⁷Behold his bed, which is Solomon's; threescore valiant men are about it, of the valiant of Israel.

⁸They all hold swords, being expert in war: every man hath his sword upon his thigh because of fear in the night.

⁹King Solomon made himself a chariot of the wood of Lebanon.

¹⁰He made the pillars thereof of silver, the bottom thereof of gold, the covering of it of purple, the midst thereof being paved with love, for the daughters of Jerusalem.

[11]Go forth, O ye daughters of Zion, and behold King Solomon with the crown wherewith his mother crowned him in the day of his espousals, and in the day of the gladness of his heart.

This chapter starts by revealing how this special lady longs to be with the focus of her heart. Her soul always desires to be near him and see him. This is how it should be when two are committed to love. She presents a metaphorical picture of seeking her love "about the city" and asking if he has been seen (verses 1-3). When he is found, she holds him and will not let him go (verse 4).

The rest of the chapter presents strong and attractive descriptions of her love, King Solomon.

Chapter 4

[1]Behold, thou art fair, my love; behold, thou art fair; thou hast doves' eyes within thy locks: thy hair is as a flock of goats that appear from mount Gilead.

[2]Thy teeth are like a flock of sheep that are even shorn, which came up from the washing; whereof every one bear twins, and none is barren among them.

[3]Thy lips are like a thread of scarlet, and thy speech is comely: thy temples are like a piece of a pomegranate within thy locks.

[4]Thy neck is like the tower of David built for an armory, whereon there hang a thousand bucklers, all shields of mighty men.

[5]Thy two breasts are like two young roes that are twins, which feed among the lilies.

[6]Until the day break, and the shadows flee away, I will get me to the mountain of myrrh, and to the hill of frankincense.

[7]Thou art all fair, my love; there is no spot in thee.

[8]Come with me from Lebanon, my spouse, with me from Lebanon: look from the top of Amana, from the top of Shenir and Hermon, from the lions' dens, from the mountains of the leopards.

[9]Thou hast ravished my heart, my sister, my spouse; thou hast ravished my heart with one of thine eyes, with one chain of thy neck.

[10]How fair is thy love, my sister, my spouse! How much better is thy love than wine! And the smell of thine ointments than all spices!

[11]Thy lips, O my spouse, drop as the honeycomb: honey and milk are under thy tongue; and the smell of thy garments is like the smell of Lebanon.

[12]A garden enclosed is my sister, my spouse; a spring shut up, a fountain sealed.

[13]Thy plants are an orchard of pomegranates, with pleasant fruits; camphire (fragrant henna), with spikenard,

[14]Spikenard and saffron; calamus (sweet cane) and cinnamon, with all trees of frankincense; myrrh and aloes, with all the chief spices:

[15]A fountain of gardens, a well of living waters, and streams from Lebanon.

[16]Awake, O north wind; and come, thou south; blow upon my garden that the spices thereof may flow out. Let my beloved come into his garden, and eat his pleasant fruits (KJV).

This chapter is filled with several love compliments, so let's get to them. Solomon tells his precious woman twice how fair she is (verse 1). Women never get tired of hearing how lovely, pretty, darling, or beautiful they are. Keep this in thought men, and release it from your mind and your mouth often in a gentle and convincing tone.

Take time to slowly and carefully to read verses 2-7, and you will see how Solomon describes her beauty. These are classic portrayals of her complete beauty. He is determined to exalt the overall beauty of his treasure of "love from Above." When he honors her, he honors her as God's gift.

Most husbands don't verbally comment often on the loveliness of their wives. Instead, they just give a nod of approval or a casual smile. Sometimes men wonder how attractive their sweetheart will be in her middle and later years. They forget that constant verbal approval and spending quality time with the one they married reduces stress, and stress reduction fights inner and outer aging. Making love to the heart with carefully selected words leads to an abundant love life.

In verse 9, he states that his spouse has ravished his heart (made it beat faster). He refers to her love as beautiful and that her love is better than wine and the fragrance of oils (verse10). Next he says her lips drip honey, and that milk and honey are under her tongue (verse 11). This last verse indicates that Solomon improvised with his kisses. What a blessed lady. They must have had lots of romantic kisses.

This man cannot quit talking about how fantastic his bride is, for he continues to speak of her pleasant overall being. He goes on to describe his bride as a garden. Descriptions used are tasty pomegranates with pleasant fruits, and spikenard, an oil with a strong, lasting fragrance (verses 12-13).

Solomon continues to bless his wife with compliments referring to her appealing aroma. More spices and oils are used in verse 14, and in the end he writes "with all the chief spices." This means she is a beautiful and fragrant wife that is the epitome of desire for his eyes and heart.

She is then described as a fountain of gardens, meaning her beauty is so vast that one beauty garden is not sufficient to contain her beauty. The well of living waters and streams of

Lebanon are clean waters that give life to people and the crops, spices, vines, and trees cited in this chapter (verse 15).

After thoroughly expanding on her beauty, verse 16 finds his bride calling upon the wind to blow through her fragrant garden and have the spices flow out to her beloved. The sole purpose is that her aroma may capture his senses. When done, he will come to "his garden of pleasure" and eat (love) his pleasant fruits.

We are only half way through this letter of love, because there are four more chapters in this uniquely preserved writing that we will explore in the next chapter. From what we have observed, we can conclude that this is a love song sung by two lovers: King Solomon and his Shulamite bride. And good news awaits us. Solomon has more about love for us to understand from God's perspective in the last half of this "romantic love book."

They prepare for any bad spiritual weather,
Experiencing the joy of spending time together.
Agreement is found in needs of correction,
Continuing to cherish each other with affection.

9

Always Cherish Each
Other for Marital Growth

Each day opens with opportunities to express love in a variety of ways. These opportunities vary because we have different desires that need to be nurtured in a marriage. As we look at the last four chapters of Solomon's love song, it will be obvious that he is deeply in love with his eye-captivating wife, one he sees as a heavenly gift of love from the God of love.

Solomon's devoted love for his bride has her drawn to him, as verse descriptions will reveal. Some word pictures that were previously mentioned will be repeated, because words of love that bless, edify, and esteem another are always accepted throughout a lifetime of marriage.

Chapter 5

[1]I am come into my garden, my sister, my spouse: I have gathered my myrrh with my

spice; I have eaten my honeycomb with my honey; I have drunk my wine with my milk: eat, O friends; drink, yea, drink abundantly, O beloved.

[2]I sleep, but my heart waketh: it is the voice of my beloved that knocketh, saying, Open to me, my sister, my love, my dove, my undefiled: for my head is filled with dew, and my locks with the drops of the night.

[3]I have put off my coat; how shall I put it on? I have washed my feet; how shall I defile them?

[4]My beloved put in his hand by the hole of the door, and my heart yearned for him.

[5]I rose up to open to my beloved; and my hands dropped with myrrh, and my fingers with sweet smelling myrrh, upon the handles of the lock.

[6]I opened to my beloved; but my beloved had withdrawn himself, and was gone: my soul failed when he spake: I sought him, but I could not find him; I called him, but he gave me no answer.

[7]The watchmen that went about the city found me, they smote me, they wounded me; the keepers of the walls took away my veil from me.

⁸I charge you, O daughters of Jerusalem, if ye find my beloved, that ye tell him, that I am sick of love (lovesick).

⁹What is thy beloved more than another beloved, O thou fairest among women? What is thy beloved more than another beloved that thou dost so charge us?

¹⁰My beloved is white and ruddy, the chiefest among ten thousand.

¹¹His head is as the most fine gold, his locks are bushy, and black as a raven.

¹²His eyes are as the eyes of doves by the rivers of waters, washed with milk, and fitly set.

¹³His cheeks are as a bed of spices, as sweet flowers: his lips like lilies, dropping sweet smelling myrrh.

¹⁴His hands are as gold rings set with the beryl: his belly is as bright ivory overlaid with sapphires.

¹⁵His legs are as pillars of marble, set upon sockets of fine gold: his countenance is as Lebanon, excellent as the cedars.

¹⁶His mouth is most sweet: yea, he is altogether lovely. This is my beloved, and this is my friend, O daughters of Jerusalem.

The first eight verses present "sense" spices such as, myrrh, wine, honeycomb, and milk to enhance their love. She waits for her beloved to arrive and then goes looking for him, for she is lovesick.

In verse 10, she begins describing her beloved and continues till the end of the chapter. Her list shows how carefully she has noticed all of her handsome man. The numerous and detailed descriptions that are cited show this bride delights in her husband from his head down to his legs. Her eyes and words celebrate his appeal. Husbands and wives should take note of this, and tell each other of their appealing beauty that is constantly before them.

Chapter 6

[1]Whither is thy beloved gone, O thou fairest among women? Whither is thy beloved turned aside that we may seek him with thee?

[2]My beloved is gone down into his garden, to the beds of spices, to feed in the gardens, and to gather lilies.

[3]I am my beloved's, and my beloved is mine: he feedeth among the lilies.

[4]Thou art beautiful, O my love, as Tirzah, comely as Jerusalem, terrible as an army with banners.

⁵Turn away thine eyes from me, for they have overcome me: thy hair is as a flock of goats that appear from Gilead.

⁶Thy teeth are as a flock of sheep which go up from the washing, whereof every one beareth twins, and there is not one barren among them.

⁷As a piece of a pomegranate are thy temples within thy locks.

⁸There are threescore queens, and fourscore concubines, and virgins without number.

⁹My dove, my undefiled is but one; she is the only one of her mother, she is the choice one of her that bare her. The daughters saw her, and blessed her; yea, the queens and the concubines, and they praised her.

¹⁰Who is she that looketh forth as the morning, fair as the moon, clear as the sun, and as awesome as an army with banners?

¹¹I went down into the garden of nuts to see the fruits of the valley, and to see whether the vine flourished, and the pomegranates budded.

¹²Or ever I was aware, my soul made me like the chariots of Amminadib (my noble people).

¹³Return, return, O Shulamite; return, return, that we may look upon thee. What will ye see in

the Shulamite? As it were the company of two armies.

In verses 4-13, Solomon again shows his love for the precious "bride of beauty" that God has brought into his heart. He praises these specifics of her appearance: her eyes and hair (verse 5), her white teeth (verse 6), the red on her temples (verse 7). He says his "darling dove of purity" is very unique and praised by many women (verses 8-9). He compares her beauty to the dawning of a day, a full moon, pure sunlight, and an awesome army carrying banners (verse 10).

If you think Solomon is finished complimenting his bride, the next chapter steps up his recognition of her undeniable and captivating beauty. New notes of beauty come forth.

Chapter 7

[1]How beautiful are thy feet with shoes, O prince's daughter! The joints of thy thighs are like jewels, the work of the hands of a cunning workman.

[2]Thy navel is like a round goblet, which wanteth not liquor: thy belly is like a heap of wheat set about with lilies.

[3]Thy two breasts are like two young roes that are twins.

[4]Thy neck is as a tower of ivory; thine eyes like the pools in Heshbon, by the gate of

Bathrabbim: thy nose is as the tower of Lebanon which looketh toward Damascus.

[5]Thine head upon thee is like Carmel, and the hair of thine head like purple (threads); the king is held in the galleries.

[6]How fair and how pleasant art thou, O love, for delights!

[7]This thy stature is like to a palm tree, and thy breasts to clusters of grapes.

[8]I said, I will go up to the palm tree, I will take hold of the boughs thereof: now also thy breasts shall be as clusters of the vine, and the smell of thy nose like apples;

[9]And the roof of thy mouth like the best wine for my beloved, that goeth down sweetly, causing the lips of those that are asleep to speak.

[10]I am my beloved's, and his desire is toward me.

[11]Come, my beloved, let us go forth into the field; let us lodge in the villages.

[12]Let us get up early to the vineyards; let us see if the vine flourish, whether the tender grape appear, and the pomegranates bud forth: there will I give thee my love.

[13]The mandrakes give a smell, and at our gates are all manner of pleasant fruits, new and old, which I have laid up for thee, O my beloved.

Immediately Solomon acknowledges the beauty of her feet in shoes, and that her thighs are the work of a talented artist (verse 1). Throughout the entire chapter, he describes her overall beauty that he beholds. I will not go into expository explanation about what he says. Read it and realize that this is a man who deeply loves his bride, spirit, soul, and body.

If husbands would observe the many beauty areas of their wives and tell them throughout the marriage of how attractive they are, the wife would desire her man of compliments more often. This chapter is a compliment guideline for both to follow so that ultimate fulfillment awaits time and time again.

Verses 12-13 show the diversity of passion in marriage with agreement. Intimate love has no bedroom boundaries.

Chapter 8

[1]O that thou wert as my brother that nursed the breasts of my mother! When I should find thee without, I would kiss thee; yea, I should not be despised.

[2]I would lead thee, and bring thee into my mother's house, who would instruct me: I would cause thee to drink of spiced wine of the juice of my pomegranate.

[3]His left hand should be under my head, and his right hand should embrace me.

[4]I charge you, O daughters of Jerusalem, that ye stir not up, nor awake my love, until he please.

[5]Who is this that cometh up from the wilderness, leaning upon her beloved? I raised thee up under the apple tree: there thy mother brought thee forth: there she brought thee forth that bare thee.

[6]Set me as a seal upon thine heart, as a seal upon thine arm: for love is strong as death; jealousy is cruel as the grave: the coals thereof are coals of fire, which hath a most vehement flame.

[7]Many waters cannot quench love, neither can the floods drown it: if a man would give all the substance (wealth) of his house for love, it would utterly be contemned (despised).

[8]We have a little sister, and she hath no breasts: what shall we do for our sister in the day when she shall be spoken for?

[9]If she be a wall, we will build upon her a palace of silver: and if she be a door, we will enclose her with boards of cedar.

[10]I am a wall, and my breasts like towers: then was I in his eyes as one that found favor.

[11]Solomon had a vineyard at Baalhamon; he let out the vineyard unto keepers; every one for the fruit thereof was to bring a thousand pieces of silver.

[12]My vineyard, which is mine, is before me: thou, O Solomon, must have a thousand, and those that keep the fruit thereof two hundred.

[13]Thou that dwellest in the gardens, the companions hearken to thy voice: cause me to hear it.

[14]Make haste, my beloved, and be thou like to a roe or to a young hart upon the mountains of spices (KJV).

I will not go into detail on the first five verses, so our focus will start on verses 6-7. These two verses have much to say about true love, a love that will not be broken or shattered. A seal of the cherished is to be set on the heart. If done, then your love for that one will be well-known. It would be like having the seal of the name of your love on your arm for all to see. This would send a "hands off of my beloved" message to all.

Various ongoing details of reciprocated and determined love have been revealed in the previous 7 chapters. Therefore, no more information or precise explanations of remaining verses in this chapter are needed to capture God's approved romance that He desires for a husband and wife.

This Song of Solomon's poetic love description is graphic, and discretion should be used when exposing it to young people. Consider their age and overall maturity. The details can easily stimulate thoughts that could lead to sensuality, which results in sexual activity. If your child has a Bible and happens to read it and asks questions, be prepared to take time to answer all questions.

King Solomon sure knew how to *cherish* his woman with "love from Above" that came from his heart, shone forth from his eyes, and flowed out of his mouth. Also, this lovely Shulamite lady gave her handsome husband the same, a heart filled with God's love and a mouth that sang the praises of gratitude. Truly, King Solomon and his bride found the spiritual journey that led to authentic love. They followed this cherish definition:

> hold dear, treat tenderly with care and
> affection, keep in mind, cling to in thought

Is your spiritual journey leading you to cherish your spouse? Consider reading Song of Songs together to enrich your relationship.

Many people will celebrate a holiday,
Not realizing His immeasurable worth.
Failing to observe God's heavenly way,
Still denying the virginity of Christ's birth.

10

A Birth to Cherish

The birth of Jesus is the most discussed birth in history. His birth has been the center of many discussions for centuries. Jesus was born in Bethlehem, a small city located in Israel. So what makes His birth so controversial? This question will be answered with startling prophetic details.

Accurate historical evidence will show God had a unique plan to enter our world thousands of years ago in human form. By doing this, His impact would change millions of lives. As information is presented, the meaning of "cherish" should be active in our heart and mind.

Old Testament prophets had a relationship with God that He ordained. No person could decide to be a prophet who represented the Almighty God unless chosen by God. A true prophet had to be 100% accurate in all that was declared as coming from God. We will look at what some of the prophets had to say about a baby that would change history forever.

In Isaiah 7:14, the prophet makes a prediction about a birth that would be heart-captivating, a unique birth that would forever change history. This prophecy reads:

> Therefore the Lord himself shall give you a
> sign; Behold, a virgin shall conceive, and bear a
> son, and shall call his name Immanuel (KJV).

These words contain specific insight into a coming event that had not ever happened. They describe a woman, who is a virgin, and she will conceive and give birth to a son. But how can a woman conceive without a man taking part in the process? Before answering this question, the word used for "virgin" must be clarified.

The Hebrew word for virgin in Isaiah 7:14 is *'almāh*. It is used to describe a virgin or a maiden. It is always used of a woman who has not borne a child.[1] This word is also used in Song of Songs 6:8 where the definition of it clearly refers to virgin women. Some have argued that since *'almāh*, could mean maiden, this means the woman described in this verse may have not been a virgin. They are wrong.

Look back at the verse and notice the last phrase, "and shall call his name Immanuel." The name Immanuel means "God with us." The son of this virgin shall carry the title of divinity. A woman, who is not a virgin, would not be chosen by God to bear this unique Person.

Matthew 1:23 clarifies any confusion about Isaiah 7:14:

> Behold, a virgin shall be with child, and shall
> bring forth a son, and they shall call his name
> Emmanuel, which being interpreted is, God
> with us (KJV).

A Birth to Cherish

Matthew was an apostle of Jesus and spent at least three years in ministry with Him. All the apostles were taught by Jesus about the Law of Moses, what the prophets foretold, and what the Psalms said concerning the coming of Israel's redeeming Messiah (Luke 24:44-45).

Definitely, Matthew understood Isaiah 7:14. The word he used for "virgin" in chapter 1, verse 23, is *parthenos*. It is also used in a parable found in Matthew 25:1-13 for women who are virgins. Luke 1:27 confirms Matthew's selection of *parthenos* in describing Mary as a "virgin."[2]

Some have wondered how a woman could conceive without having sex. In this case, it's very simple. The Almighty God, Who spoke the world into existence out of nothing (Genesis 1), could easily speak to the womb of the woman and cause her egg to be fertilized and bring forth life. The Holy Spirit caused this miraculous conception to occur (Matthew 1:18-20; Luke 1:34-35).

A correction about the Virgin Mary's lifestyle needs our understanding. Some have been taught that she remained a virgin all her life and never had any children. The Bible says otherwise. Matthew 12:46-47, 13:55-56, Mark 6:3, and Luke 8:19-21 all mention that Mary had sons and daughters from her husband Joseph. These children were conceived in normal love between a husband and a wife *after* Christ's virgin birth. There is no verse that says these sons and daughters were Joseph's from a previous marriage.

Another prophecy about the birth of Christ has amazing content. It is found in Micah 5:2 and reads:

> But as for you, Bethlehem Ephrathah, Too little
> to be among the clans of Judah, from you One
> will go forth for Me to be ruler in Israel. His
> goings forth are from long ago, from the days of
> eternity (NASB).

This prophecy tells where Jesus would be born about 700 hundred years in advance, in the town of Bethlehem (Matthew 2:1). Also, He is from the tribe of Judah, and His existence is "from the days of eternity." The Hebrew word for "eternity" in this verse is *ôlâm* and is used often in the Old Testament to describe the eternal God, as cited in Psalm 90:2.

If Jesus' days are from eternity, that means He existed before His birth in Bethlehem. Here is where the uniqueness of Christ is magnified. His human nature had a beginning when He was conceived in the Virgin Mary. However, human nature cannot exist from eternity. So what does the phrase "from the days of eternity" mean? It refers to His nature He had in Heaven, and this nature was with Him while on the earth.

In John's Gospel, Jesus claims to be both the Son of God (John 3:16; 5:25) and the Son of man in John 5:27. Why does Jesus make this "compound claim" about Himself? He is declaring to those who are listening that there are two full and complete natures within Him, the nature of God and the nature of man. The phrase "Son of God" defines His eternal divine nature. The phrase "Son of man" defines His human nature that came into existence when He was conceived in Mary. Two natures in one Person is hard to understand, but it's Biblical.

A Birth to Cherish

Biblical teaching about the two full and complete natures of Christ has caused much controversy for centuries, but it is taught in Micah 5:2 as previously shown. Another verse, Isaiah 9:6, teaches the two natures of the coming "Prince of peace." It was foretold about 700 years before Jesus was born. It reads:

> For unto us a child is born, unto us a son is given: and the government shall be upon his shoulder: and his name shall be called Wonderful, Counsellor, The mighty God, The everlasting Father, The Prince of Peace (KJV).

The phrase "unto us a child is born" represents the human nature (virgin birth). The phrase "unto us a son is given" identifies the eternal divine nature of God's Son, which is from everlasting as Micah 5:2 foretold. This demonstrates another clear example of two natures in one man. These two separate natures, human and divine in one Person, explain why Jesus is often called "the God-man."

John's Gospel was the last Gospel written. God wanted the world to know something very important, so He inspired John to write this powerful Gospel that definitely portrays the Deity (eternal nature) of Jesus. The two natures of Christ are clearly stated in the first chapter (John 1:1-3, 14).

> [1]In the beginning was the Word, and the Word was with God, and the Word was God. [2]The same was in the beginning with God. [3]All things

> were made by him; and without him was not anything made that was made.... [14]And the Word was made flesh, and dwelt among us, (and we beheld his glory, the glory as of the only begotten of the Father,) full of grace and truth (KJV).

In verse 1, Jesus is called "the Word," and "the Word" was God. Verse 2 shows that He is separate and distinct from His Father, and yet He also is referred to as God. These two verses are used to explain the Trinity or Triune nature of the one God Who exists eternally as three separate Persons of the same nature. They represent the God of the Bible. The Holy Spirit is the third Person of the Trinity. Jesus gives insight to the personal work of the Holy Spirit in John, chapters 14-16.

Jesus, along with His Father, is given credit for making (creating) all things in verse 3. The apostle Paul also gives credit to Jesus for creating all things in Colossians 1:16, and says "He is before all things" in verse 17. The One Who is before all things takes part in creating all things.

John 1:14 says the Word (Jesus) was made flesh (the virgin birth) and dwelt among mankind. From verse 1 to verse 14, it never says the Word (Jesus) left His divine nature in Heaven. God became a man through the virgin birth, and more vital information must be presented from Matthew, chapter 1, and Luke, chapters 1-3, to explain why God became a man. These two Gospels show how the virgin birth is connected to God's plan to redeem man and forgive all our sins.

A Birth to Cherish

Matthew 1:21 says "you shall call His name Jesus, for He shall save His people from their sins." Keep in mind the phrase "save His people from their sins." Luke was a beloved physician (Colossians 4:14) and was known for his details when presenting facts. Numerous facts become evident as we delve into his first two chapters of his Gospel.

Luke 1:26-35 gives an account of an angel's visit to the Virgin Mary. At the end of verse 35, the angel tells Mary that "her holy offspring shall be called the Son of God." On His eighth day, Jesus was brought to Jerusalem to be presented to the LORD (chapter 2, verses 21-22). A man named Simeon came to the temple (verses 25-27), took Jesus in his arms and prophesied the following:

> [28]then he took Him into his arms, and blessed God, and said, [29]"Now Lord, You are releasing Your bond-servant to depart in peace, According to Your word; [30]For my eyes have seen Your salvation, [31]Which You have prepared in the presence of all peoples, [32]A LIGHT OF REVELATION TO THE GENTILES, And the glory of Your people Israel" (NASB).

Verse 32 unlocks God's will for all the world. The salvation his eyes had seen (verse 30) was the baby Jesus, and He would one day bring the light of revelation and truth to the hearts of the Gentiles so that they also could have forgiveness.

The Jewish people proved to be the vehicle by which God would proclaim forgiveness to the nations of the world (Matthew 28:18-20).

Romans 5:12 teaches that sin entered humanity through one man (Adam). This refers to Adam's sin in the Garden of Eden, which was eating of the forbidden fruit from a specific tree (Genesis 3:1-12). Verse 6 reveals Eve rebelled by eating the fruit. Adam was with her and did nothing to stop her from violating God's command (verse 3).

Adam was created first. This gave him the responsibility to lead Eve in God's way. When he allowed her to violate God's instruction, he sinned before she did, because he did nothing to prevent her from eating the fruit. Verse 6 says "her husband was with her." Therefore, from the first man, Adam, God chose to pass down sin to all people at conception.

King David wrote that "in sin did my mother conceive me" (Psalm 51:5). This means we are all born into a nature of sin. At what age a person becomes accountable to God for sinning is up for debate. The good news is that God sent His Son to be the One to forgive our sins.

This is why the virgin birth happened. Since the sinful seed of man is passed on when conception occurs, then in order to bypass the transfer of sin, God miraculously caused the Virgin Mary to conceive without the seed of man entering her to cause her to be pregnant.

In the final chapter, more specifics on how to be assured that your sins are forgiven, removed, and will *never* (Psalm 103:12) be remembered by God will be outlined. The perfect life Jesus lived will be explained to understand why He had to live a life with no sin for us (1 Peter 2:22).

Though we do not know the exact day Jesus was born, His birth is celebrated annually in December around the world by millions, maybe over a billion people. Millions sing songs about Him at church services or daily during this month. Many visit senior retirement homes to sing for the elderly. Manger scenes are displayed around the world during the Christmas season, and plays are presented that re-enact His birth.

Some, who don't know their Bible well, have said it is wrong to celebrate Jesus at Christmas, because we don't know the exact day He was born. They are wrong. God was prepared for this unbiblical attitude in the first century when he had the apostle Paul write Romans 14:5-8 where it says it is okay to regard one day above another when honoring the LORD.

Remember earlier in the chapter when Isaiah 9:6 was mentioned? The last part of the verse describes Jesus as the "Prince of peace." What great comfort to know Someone Who truly gives peace to your heart (John 14:27). This precious baby changed the world. He was not an ordinary baby, but an extraordinary supernatural baby Who came into the world with "love from Above." We are His beloved and treasured holy possessions. We must always cherish Him in our hearts.

Faith Hill is a lovely lady with a fantastic voice. She recorded a song titled *A Baby Changes Everything*. It is about the Virgin Mary and what she experiences with her baby Jesus. Please listen to the song before you read the next chapter. It's found on YouTube.

A Baby Changes Everything

Teenage girl, much too young
Unprepared for what's to come
A baby changes everything

Not a ring on her hand
All her dreams and all her plans
A baby changes everything
A baby changes everything

The man she loves she's never touched
How will she keep his trust?
A baby changes everything
A baby changes everything

And she cries!
Ooh, she cries
Ooh, oh

She has to leave, go far away
Heaven knows she can't stay
A baby changes everything

She can feel it's coming soon
There's no place, there's no room
A baby changes everything
A baby changes everything

A Birth to Cherish

And she cries!
And she cries!
Oh, she cries

Shepherds all gather 'round
Up above the star shines down
A baby changes everything

Choir of angels sing
Glory to the newborn King
A baby changes everything
A baby changes everything
Everything, everything, everything

Hallelujah
Hallelujah
Hallelujah
Hallelujah

My whole life has turned around
I was lost but now I'm found
A baby changes everything, yeah
A baby changes everything

After listening to this song, how much has the birth of Jesus entering history changed your life? Are you one of the millions who sing songs of admiration to Him? If not, will you become one who does? Have you permitted Him to come into your life to know the "Prince of peace" in a special way?

Chapter 2 of Luke's Gospel presents more details of the miraculous night Jesus was born. Verses 8-12 state that an angel appeared to shepherds at night while they were watching their flock. The glory of God shone around them. The angel told them he "brought good tidings of great joy," namely that born this day was a Savior in the city of David, Who is Christ the Lord.

Verses 13-14 give us a heavenly picture of a multitude of angels praising God and saying "Glory to God in the highest, and on earth peace among those with whom He is pleased." After the angels left, the men went to Bethlehem to find the most precious child ever to be born. Such a spectacular birth was prophetically designed according to previous Scriptures presented in this chapter. No baby has ever had a glorious entrance in history like Jesus.

Now let's look at a list of facts that are very important concerning the virgin birth, because this one-of-a-kind birth has never been duplicated in history.

- If Jesus was not born of a virgin, then the New Testament records are false and unreliable.
- If Jesus was not born of a virgin, then Christ was not born of the seed of a woman (Genesis 3:15), but born of the sinful seed passed on by a man.
- If Jesus was not born of a virgin, then He was not the Son of God, but a physical son of some man.
- If Jesus was not born of a virgin, then He is a sinner like all people, and spent His life deceiving people by claiming to be God's Son (John 10:36).

- If Jesus was not born of a virgin, we have no Savior (Luke 2:11).
- If Jesus was not born of a virgin, Mary brought an illegitimate child into the world with a sinful encounter with an unknown man.[3]

Old and New Testament verses establish the virgin birth of Jesus, as the Son of God. A verse from 1 Timothy 3:16 sheds more light on the Deity of Jesus, as God in the flesh.

> And without controversy great is the mystery of godliness: *God was manifest in the flesh* (my emphasis), justified in the Spirit, seen of angels, preached unto the Gentiles, believed on in the world, received up into glory (KJV).

This verse speaks volumes of information about the Son of God. He was God in human flesh, because His divine nature came from Heaven to take flesh upon it. The next chapter will reveal another miracle about Jesus that shocked the world.

Endnotes:

1. W. E. Vine, Merrill F. Unger, William White Jr., *Vine's Complete Expository Dictionary of Old and New Testament Words*, (Nashville, Tennessee, Thomas Nelson Publishers, 1985), pp. 276-277.

2. Ibid., p. 661.

3. D. James Kennedy, *Solving Bible Mysteries* (Nashville, Tennessee, Thomas Nelson Publishers, 2000), pp. 52-53.

Stretched on a cross gasping for breath,
Increasing agony desires to conquer death.
A body streams forgiveness with Holy blood,
For His gift of love will purify all like a flood.

11

A Death and
Resurrection to Cherish

Rising from the dead is no easy task. How can this be done, if it is possible? Has anyone done it successfully and lived on after being dead for days in a tomb, and then appeared to hundreds of people to prove that he was raised physically from the dead? Specific historical facts will be laid out to answer these vital questions.

In the last chapter, prophecies foretelling Christ's birth in Bethlehem and that He is from everlasting (Micah 5:2), that He would carry the title of "God with us" (Isaiah 7:14), and His two natures in one person (Isaiah 9:6) label His entrance into history as unparalleled. But there is more excitement to unveil as we look at His prophetic death and His history-changing physical resurrection.

Like His prophetic birth, there are prophecies hundreds of years before the Son of God came to earth that describe how He would die and overcome death. These prophecies show spectacular details about how He would be put to death. They also foretell His resurrection after He was dead and buried.

The way Jesus would be crucified was described in Psalm 22 during the time of King David, which was hundreds of years before the Messiah was born in Bethlehem. These crucifixion prophecies refer *only* to the Savior Who will forgive our sins.

> [7]All who see me sneer at me; They separate with
> the lip, they wag the head, saying,

Notice the word "sneer" in verse 7. In Luke 23:35, the rulers are "sneering" at Jesus while He suffers on the cross, not knowing they are fulfilling a prophecy spoken centuries ago. Mark 15:29-31 paints a graphic picture of who was doing the sneering (mocking). They were Gentiles, chief priests, and scribes who had heard Jesus preach and saw Him do miracles of healing for three years. But this meant nothing to them.

> [14]I am poured out like water, And all my bones
> are out of joint; My heart is like wax; It is
> melted within me.
>
> [15]My strength is dried up like a potsherd, And
> my tongue cleaves to my jaws; And You lay me
> in the dust of death.
>
> [16]For dogs have surrounded me; A band of
> evildoers has encompassed me; They pierced
> my hands and my feet.
>
> [17]I can count all my bones. They look, they stare
> at me;

A Death and Resurrection to Cherish

Verses 14-17 describe how, when God's Son would be nailed to the cross, His joints would slowly be ripped apart during His hours of suffering before death. He would become dehydrated from the ongoing and intense anguish He was suffering. Blood would be running from the crown of thorns pressed upon His head. The horrible beating and scourging He experienced before being nailed to the cross (Mark 15:15-19) would cause blood to cover His body.

When these Psalm 22 verses were recorded, crucifixion was not a form of death punishment. But God knew the future and how His Son would be crucified for the sins of humanity. Jesus would "taste death for every person" (Hebrews 2:9). Because of His brutal beating, scourging, and suffering on the cross, His appearance was marred more than any man (Isaiah 52:14).

The sentence "They pierced My hands and My feet" (verse 16) correlates with Isaiah 53:5 where it says, "He was pierced through for our transgressions." The dogs mentioned in this verse are described as "evildoers," because they had no remorse for the pain and brutal suffering this innocent Man experienced.

> [18]They divide my garments among them, And
> for my clothing they cast lots (NASB).

Just as predicted in verse 18, it was fulfilled while Jesus was dying on the cross (John 19:23-24). So many details prophesied about this unique death cannot be a coincidence.

The death of Jesus deserves scrutiny, because according to information from different eye witness sources, He did not remain in the tomb after He was dead.

In John 2:19-21, Jesus foretold His own physical resurrection. In a confrontation, He told some Jews this: "Destroy this temple, and in three days I will raise it up" (KJV). When He made this statement, Jesus was referring to His body being raised from the dead. He was not saying that He would destroy the Jewish temple and rebuild it in three days.

While on the cross, He was mocked and ridiculed (Matthew 27:39-40) for making this profound prediction. We will now inspect the words of Jesus concerning raising up His temple (body). His declaration of His physical resurrection and fulfillment would launch a wave of His love and forgiveness throughout the Roman Empire.

After Jesus died on the cross, His body was wrapped in linen (Mark 15:46) that contained a mixture of myrrh and aloes (John 19:39-40). The tomb, where He was placed, was "hewn out of rock," and a large stone was rolled against the entrance of the tomb (Matthew 27:60).

This one-of-a-kind resurrection story is prophesied in Psalm 16:10. The second part of this verse says that "God would not allow His Holy One to undergo decay." To know what this statement truly means, we will learn from the apostle Peter whom Jesus taught personally for three years.

Who is God's Holy One? It refers to *only* one person. God's Holy One is His Holy Son sent from Heaven. Even the demons knew Jesus was the Holy One. In Mark 1:22-26, Jesus is teaching in a synagogue. A demon screams in rage and fear, admitting that Jesus is "the Holy One of God." Jesus cast out the unclean spirit from the man. However, Jesus' power over demons is not what God wants us to recognize as the key to knowing Jesus is "the Holy One of God."

In Acts, chapter 2, the Holy Spirit comes from Heaven upon the apostles and empowers them to preach the Gospel (good news) about Jesus. Peter declares a message filled with prophetic information (verses 16-23) to prepare his audience for the most powerful claim he could make about Jesus. Peter says God raised Jesus from the dead (verse 24), because "it was impossible for death to hold Him in its grip."

As Peter continued to astound the crowd with facts about the Lord Jesus, he said that God would not allow "His Holy One to undergo decay" (verse 27). Peter was quoting from Psalm 16:10. He explains "the Holy One of God" theme in verses 31 and 32 by preaching Jesus' body did not decay in a tomb but was raised from the dead. Peter also proclaimed that we (the apostles with him) were eyewitnesses to the Christ's resurrection.

Several faithful women were also witnesses of seeing their Lord alive after He spent three days dead, wrapped in linen with spices in the tomb (Matthew 28:1-9; Mark 16:1-10; Luke 23:55-56; 24:1-10; John 20:1-18). These ladies of love and service were at the tomb of Christ to witness the empty tomb before any of the apostles. These women truly had a heart of appreciation and love for the Lord Jesus. All four Gospels include the story of Christ's crucifixion and resurrection.

The story of Christ's physical resurrection is told throughout *The Book of Acts*, a book that records decades of trips to various areas by the apostles telling the world of God's forgiveness of their sins. The importance of the resurrection is emphasized in multiple places in the Bible.

In Matthew 27:51-53, we find that tombs/graves, other than the tomb of Jesus, were opened and many *bodies* of the saints were raised. Coming out of the tombs *after* Christ's resurrection, they entered the holy city and appeared to many people. Such an event certainly changed people's lives.

Paul wrote in Romans 1:4 that "Jesus is declared to be the Son of God with power according to the Spirit of holiness, by His resurrection from the dead." The resurrection truly makes the life and death of Jesus the story of all stories.

First Corinthians 15:1-9 mentions different groups of people who saw Jesus alive after He was raised from the dead. Verse 6 reveals that He appeared to over 500 at one time, most of whom were still alive when Paul wrote this epistle. All of those who saw Jesus after His death and resurrection could not have been fooled by an imposter.

To stress the reality and importance of the resurrection, Paul told the Corinthians in verses 12-17 that if Christ has not been raised from the dead and there is no resurrection, their faith is worthless, and they are still in their sins. Without the resurrection of God's Son, there would be no Christianity.

John 11:1-45 teaches an amazing miracle that Jesus did. His friend Lazarus had been dead four days (verse 39). Jesus raised him from the dead (verses 43-44). In verse 25, Jesus said

"I am the resurrection and the life. He who believes in Me shall live, even if he dies" (NASB). He proved it by raising Lazarus from the dead. This Jewish time of mourning became a time of public praise.

Many skeptics have tried to refute the resurrection of Jesus and have come up with strange ideas. Josh McDowell, world-renowned author, has written books that expose the fallacious ideas that try to refute Christ's resurrection. Two of them are titled *The Resurrection Factor,* and *The Resurrection and You*. His thorough research shows the various arguments against the resurrection are not valid. These are valuable resource books to have.

There is no other recorded religion or faith in the world that foretold a physical resurrection of One Who would come from Heaven to die for their sins, be raised from the dead, and go back to Heaven to prepare a place for those who want to be with Him (John 14:1-3). At Easter time, millions of people sing songs commemorating His sacrifice on the cross, His death, burial, and His resurrection on Sunday, also known as "Son day," which honors the Son of God.

The early believers in Christ spread His Gospel of love like a flame. It could not be extinguished because of His love for them and their love for Him. Being cherished by "the Author of love" by example makes us want to cherish and love people like He does.

The Lord of love has prepared a heavenly place.
To live there is freely given with amazing grace.
God's City of Eternal Love has plenty of space.
All skin colors radiate His glory upon their face.
(Revelation 5:9; 7:9-12)

12

Jesus Came From
Heaven to Cherish Us

The previous chapters explained how God cherishes us, how we can cherish Him, and how we are to cherish each other. The Bible is filled with numerous examples that encourage us to live the "cherish lifestyle." Glancing back at each chapter heading refreshes what we have learned about the meaning of cherish. Therefore, daily we are to present a lifestyle of love for God and fellow man. "Love from Above" should clothe our identity.

Before Christ's earthly ministry was finished, He gave His disciples specific instructions about where their lives would branch out as they proclaimed the Gospel. The Gospel is the good news of God's love and forgiveness for all people. In Acts 1:8, He told them they would receive power when the Holy Spirit came upon them, and they would be His witnesses in Jerusalem, Judea, Samaria, and to the uttermost part of the earth. Then He ascended into Heaven (Acts 1:9-11).

In John, chapters 14-16, Jesus gave details on the power of the Holy Spirit Who would indwell them in the near future.

When Pentecost time came, which brought multitudes of Jews to Jerusalem, the Holy Spirit came upon the disciples to declare that God had sent Jesus, the Holy One, to die for their sins (Acts 2:1-41). In verse 38, Peter tells the crowd to *repent* in the Name of Jesus for the forgiveness of their sins, be baptized, and they would receive the gift of the Holy Spirit.

For understanding what God calls sins, I will list some verses that describe sins. We will look at Galatians 5:19-21, because it has several examples of why Christ died on the cross for our sins.

> [19]Now the deeds of the flesh are evident, which are: sexual immorality, impurity, sensuality, [20]idolatry, sorcery, enmities, strife, jealousy, outbursts of anger, disputes, dissensions, factions, [21]envying, drunkenness, carousing, and things like these, of which I forewarn you, just as I have forewarned you, that those who practice such things will not inherit the kingdom of God (NASB).

Exodus 20:1-17 lists other sins people commit, such as idol (demon) worship, cursing God (using His Name in vain or in any improper manner), children dishonoring their parents, murdering someone, stealing, bearing false witness (lying), and coveting another person's possessions. If we look at what Exodus 20 and Galatians 5 list as sins (rebelling against God's standard of holiness) and are honest, we have sinned (Romans

3:23) at different times during our life. Our sin leads to spiritual death (Romans 6:23). We should not disregard sin.

To cherish us by forgiving our sins is the reason Jesus came from Heaven (John 3:16). Jesus made a spiritual journey from Heaven to show His authentic love for us when He took flesh upon Himself to live among us. His prophetic death and resurrection information presented in the last chapter foretold Christ's purpose while on the earth. His mission was to redeem us by forgiving our sins and to teach us heavenly love.

Understanding how our sins are forgiven is crucial so that we can be assured of living in Heaven with God when we pass away. God has set up a specific way, outlined in Scripture, to forgive our sins, and His way is fair for all. God's way is through Christ's shed blood on the cross.

Hebrews 9:22 says "without the shedding of blood, there is no forgiveness." When explaining the New Covenant during Communion, Jesus said His shed blood represented the forgiveness of our sins (Matthew 26:27-29). Ephesians 1:7 reads:

> In whom we have redemption through His blood, the forgiveness of sins, according to the riches of His grace (KJV).

This verse confirms our blood redemption by Jesus that assures us forgiveness. The apostle Peter also stated that the followers of Christ were redeemed "with the precious blood of Christ" (1 Peter 1:18-19). When you believe in your heart that

Jesus shed His blood and died for your sins, you receive God's forgiveness, and the Holy Spirit comes to indwell you (Romans 8:9, 11). Then God places His seal of redemption upon you, as His purchased possession (Ephesians 1:13-14).

If a person is truly repentant for their sins, there is a lifestyle change that in some way exhibits Christ has come into their life, because Jesus is Holy. The change varies from person to person and exhibits the gifting and calling that the LORD inserts in each person. The Holy Spirit helps us to avoid sins that we struggle with at times during our new life in Christ. And He reminds us to confess our sins (1 John 1:9) after we have received Jesus as our Lord and Savior.

God loves us just as we are and accepts as we are when we come to Him to have our sins forgiven. We come as sinners who need the Savior, and God expects us to fight against sin *after* we receive Christ (Romans 6:12-14). We must not continue in sin with no evidence of remorse for our sins. Such a lifestyle portrays a false conversion, mocks Christ's blood, and misrepresents Christianity.

When we receive Christ, the Holy Spirit helps us resist the schemes of invisible evil spirits (Ephesians 6:10-19). We are cherished with Christ's supernatural protection. Also, holy angels protect us. Those who *have not* received Jesus as their Lord and Savior are more vulnerable to demonic influence.

As members in the Body of Christ (1 Corinthians 12:27; Ephesians 4:12), all become ambassadors for Christ with a heavenly Gospel message (2 Corinthians 5:20). Humanity needs to hear that they are cherished by God. Christ's servants are gifted in diverse ways to present God's Gospel of eternal love and forgiveness, and should always be ready to give an answer for the hope that lives within them in a gentle and reverent manner (1 Peter 3:15).

By sending His Son to die for our sins, it proves God loves and cherishes everyone (John 3:16-17). Think about this: Everyday billions of people sin many times, and God is willing to forgive everyone who admits their sins and asks Him to forgive them. So don't ever think that God doesn't love the people of His created world. He is the Savior of *all* men (1 Timothy 4:10) and desires for all to come to repentance of their sins (2 Peter 3:9), that they would experience His love.

Christ's shed blood for our sins, death on the cross, burial, and resurrection highlight the plan God set forth to guide us to Him. He removes our sins "as far as east is from west" (Psalm 103:12). Also, Micah 7:19 is good news for all, because "God treads our sins underfoot and hurls our iniquities into the depths of the sea." God is kind and good.

Those who want God's forgiveness must not ever believe their so-called good works forgive their sins, because no such teaching is found in the Bible. God's grace through Jesus forgives our sins, not our works, as stated in Ephesians 2:8-9. Our good works glorify God. To believe our good works forgive our sins is saying what Jesus did for us on the cross was not enough. Can anyone do better than Jesus?

Some believe that "all have a spark of divinity within" from child birth. To them, this means that we are automatically God's forgiven children, which is wrong. If this were true, then

Jesus wasted His time coming from Heaven to die for our sins, and Jesus lied about needing to receive Him personally to become God's children (John 1:12-13). Being saved from the eternal consequences of our sins, which separate us from God, is available by faith in Christ for His sacrificial work on the cross (1 Corinthians 15:1-8).

There is no population limit in Heaven. Only people who will not admit they have sinned and refuse to accept God's forgiveness limit the population in Heaven. Heaven will be filled with all the skin colors from the nations of our world (Revelation 5:9; 7:9-12). Every resident will be cherished forever and will make Heaven eternally beautiful. Praise the LORD for preparing Heaven for us! (John 14:1-3).

Some have wondered about those who never heard the Gospel and if they had a chance to be forgiven. There are Scriptures that shed light on this hot topic.

Psalm 19:1 says "The heavens declare the glory of God and the work of His hands." Ecclesiastes 3:11 tells us "God has set eternity in the hearts of man that they might know Him." These verses reveal that the Almighty is the One Who created all things. He has made the hearts of all people to have an awareness of Him so that He could personally cherish them.

Since God knows each heart of humanity, He knows who would have received or rejected Jesus from the beginning of time to this day if they had heard the Gospel of love before passing away. Therefore, He can judge all people in fairness, knowing whether they would have rejected or received His forgiveness for their sins.

One more subject deserves our attention. People want to know what happens to those who hear of God's love and Christ's work of forgiveness on the cross, yet reject His free offer to forgive their sins. God doesn't force anyone to go to Heaven. It's a grace opportunity.

However, God is grieved when individuals don't care about His Son "tasting death for every person" (Hebrews 2:9) and suffering a horrible death on the cross to reconcile them to His Father in Heaven. If they don't want Heaven where things are wonderful (Revelation 21:1-7), then He will let them exist away from Heaven.

Here are some descriptions of afterlife you can study if you don't want to live in Heaven when you pass away: Luke 16:19-26; Revelation 14:9-11; 20:10-15; 21:8. Read chapters 21-22 in Revelation and believe that Jesus purchased a blessed eternity for as many as received Him as Lord and Savior.

Because of one man's sin (Adam – Romans 5:12) in the Garden of Eden, humanity was driven out of the beautiful earthly paradise. Because of the blood sacrifice on the cross and sin-free life of Jesus (2 Corinthians 5:21; 1 Peter 2:22), the heavenly God-man, all have been given the gracious offering of being brought back to eternal life in God's heavenly paradise forever.

When the LORD created the world, He had a plan to cherish us, forgive our sins, and reconcile us back to His Holy presence, as stated in Revelation 13:8, where it mentions "the Lamb of God (Jesus – John 1:29) Who was slain from the foundation of the world" (KJV). Our *Cherished with Love from Above*" spiritual journey from Genesis to Revelation has revealed God's eternal love for us. God's door to eternal life and love is found when you receive and have Jesus as your personal Savior (John 1:12; 1 John 5:11-12).

Upon believing in Jesus as the Savior from your sins (Acts 4:12) and receiving His forgiveness in your heart, you are placed in His spiritual heart forever where you are loved, cherished, and treasured as His precious beloved. As members of the worldwide Body of Christ, Christians are to portray His image of love and what it means to be cherished by Jesus, "The Lord of Love." God's zip code for eternal love is John 3:16.

Will I See You In Heaven?

A Wife Writes a Cherish Note

The information that is contained in what this woman of God wrote to her husband is absolutely beautiful. The content reveals that she cherishes her husband. It is her way of reaching out to him to present her love for him so that he will cherish her in return. It is presented exactly how she wrote it.

> To my John,
>
> I want to take
>   care of you…
> I want us to
>   serve Jesus…
> I want to kiss
>   you…and hold
>   you every night.
>
> I want to share
>   my life with you…
> I want to be with
>   you in the
>   happy times…
> I want to be with
>   you in the
>   painful times…
>
> I want us to
>   hurt and grow…
>   together… closer…

with Christ.
I want your
  love…
I want us…
I want you…
  to be with
  me for
  eternity.

I love you my
  John…
I need you my
  husband…
I want you as
  our Lord promised.

I give all my
    love to
  'my John.'

I give my
  heart to you…

I give myself
    to my
Lord and my
  husband.

…eternity…

—your Lisa—

Well, what did you think of this? Was complete love and acceptance shown with these words? Was there a desire to always be alongside her husband, which was the pattern God set in the Garden of Eden? Her expressions of "love from Above" are a blessing that saturate her husband's spirit, soul, and body. Is it time for you to write a "cherish" note or letter to your spouse? Don't delay, and plan on writing more than one during your marriage. You will have an ongoing blessing.